Olle Hjern

OPEN DOORS
Swedenborg Essays

ISBN 978-91-982096-3-1

Editing: Dawn Potts & Gail Oler
Layout: Ottar Ludvigsen
Cover: Tanya Perskaya
Publisher: Edition TPW-Tornet
First Edition: 300 copies
Printing: BoD Germany 2019

Olle Hjern

OPEN DOORS
Essays on Swedenborg

**Translated from Swedish
by Susanna Åkerman-Hjern**

Editions TPW-Tornet & LNC Publishing 2019

Pastor Olle Hjern

Table of Contents:

Preface

The Reverend Olle Hjern (1926-2016), was an amazing person. For sixty years he was the compassionate pastor of the Swedenborgian Society of the Lord's New Church in Sweden. He also oversaw the Congregation of the New Church Confessors. After his theological training in Bryn Athyn, Pennsylvania, in the fifties, he was involved in not only leading societies in Stockholm, Gothenburg, Arboga and Örebro but he also traveled to Berlin, Germany, for many years as their visiting pastor. He also traveled to other Lord's New Church societies, including Durban in South Africa, Maseru in Lesotho and also Yokohama in Japan, to preach and attend gatherings.

It was his love of the arts, in all their forms, that was felt complementing his preaching. That artistic awareness touched everything of his life. His spiritually elevated speeches were wonderfully colored with deep insights and far reaching thoughts and visions from the teachings of the New Church,

During these years he wrote a series of articles on Swedenborg's influence for the New Church journal *Världarnas möte – The Meeting of Worlds*.

He also was asked to write for several American anthologies. Among his posthumous papers were found many unpublished texts giving a variety of perspectives on Swedenborg's influence. All of these fascinating articles are published here, including the history of the Skara Swedenborgians, autobiographical scenes from his own spiritual path, to Swedenborg's vision of near-death-experiences.

It is expected that these articles will be much enjoyed. Not only do they shed light on the historical development of the New Church, but they remind us of Olle's lucid activity through out his life; A life dedicated to helping all that he met to to find their spiritual sphere in the world.

This anthology has the title **Open Doors** after Olle's own motto. He was inspired by this title from the German Swedenborgian Journal, *Offene Tore*, now published in Zürich, Switzerland. Olle had also traveled there to participate in seminars.

Perhaps it was his deep and rich knowledge of many languages that enabled him to see things in multifaceted ways. He himself was always Open for new meetings with people from all walks of life, who often did seek the light and warmth of his generous spirit.

May we remember him with joy!

Historical Details of Swedenborg's Life
On Emanuel Swedenborg

Olle Hjern

"The New Church" is a title for those people in this world who in some way have let themselves be influenced by the personal heritage and the written message of the remarkable Swede, Emanuel Swedenborg (1688-1772). The term "the New Church" refers to the coming of the kingdom of God, which with all his efforts he, in the deepest sense, strove to make real. It would be a kingdom where the technical accomplishments of the new age were united with ancient spiritual wisdom and where they searched after light and revelation from the heavenly source.

Swedenborg was born in Stockholm in a pastor's home where his father, Jesper Svedberg, was court preacher and military chaplain. Svedberg was a powerful person close to the royal house and had great power and renown, but did not always conform to what was considered the correct doctrine of the day. Faith without works was no real faith, he declared. A strong personal relationship with his Divine Father he took for granted. Svedberg had high hopes for his son, Emanuel, whose earlier spiritual interests surely contributed to his parents' experience; whereby it was as if angels spoke through Emanuel's mouth.

The world of angels was always a subject of strong interest to Svedberg as was to also be the case for his son Emanuel. The father wrote many touching psalms on angels where he especially emphasized their role as guardians and movers of the intentions of Divine providence. Also, according to Svedberg's memoirs, he also experienced dreams received and honored by angels. Svedberg had the same view of the origin of angels as his son later did: They had all been human beings in this populated earthly world.

Svedberg soon became Professor of Theology in Uppsala and

then Bishop of Skara. However, he did not give up his great ambitions for his son, although Emanuel appeared to deviate from the projected theological path of studies. Certainly, the young Emanuel had been drawn to the natural sciences early on, through the private instruction he received from his slightly older friend and cousin, Johan Moreus, who was a city physician in Falun. He had inherited the family property in Sveden near Falun where Emanuel must have stayed many times and where one can still see the richly decorated wedding hall where his daughter Sara was married to the young Carl Linneaus (Carl von Linné).

Jesper Svedberg was nominated Professor of Theology at Uppsala and it was quite natural that his son Emanuel, already at nine years of age, was registered as a student at the university. There were undeniably the best private tutors, an office that professors and older students competed to receive.

In 1709, Emanuel defended a doctoral thesis on texts in Stoic philosophy, by the Roman philosophers Seneca and Publilius Syrus Mimus, plus some additions by Erasmus of Rotterdam, all in Latin and Greek, with a disputation test in Latin. Perhaps the texts had been collected by Emanuel himself, or perhaps by his professor.

Jesper, the father, was nominated Bishop in the town of Skara, in Westergötland, and here Emanuel began with intense effort and interest to study what he could find of wonderful formations in nature. He could soon discover remains of dead water animals high up on land. He was content for many years with the explanation that they were remains from Noah's Flood. Most famous is perhaps the remains of a whale encountered on the Kinnekulle hills. Also, he saw in nature the signs of an ancient vegetation in Sweden which pointed to a time there of a much warmer climate. He agreed with his old teacher Olof Rudbeck in Uppsala that we in the North once had a true paradise, when the earth then rotated faster and "golden fruits" grew profusely there. Later he also argued for something similar, but denied the connections to the literal reading of the Bible.

His name was then still Emanuel Svedberg and he could have of course, completed his studies along the lines of his father's wishes. However, his close circle of friends in Uppsala, with the brother-in-law, Eric Benzelius, as central figure would now create a collegium curiosorum, "the college of the curious", whose efforts were to collect all newer knowledge in the domains of learning and whose aims were shared by Emanuel to a high degree. He accepted to work for a longer period of time in London, England. However, in his eagerness to enter the country, he overstepped certain rules of quarantine, which could have rendered him the death penalty. The Uppsala circle's view on the King of the land was apparently rather ambivalent. However, at the time, the King was seeking all means of support for his plans on technical development. The King especially came to appreciate one of the members of the college: Christopher Polhem, the foremost engineer of our country at this time. Emanuel soon became Polhems's close assistant and they worked with technical development with various inventions - all subject to the King's interest.

The King was assisted by extraordinarily skillfully planned transports of ships on land during the war in the North, and everything indicates that he wanted to engage the young Emanuel for the continuing war. The three of them had conferred with each other in Lund and the King had given support for their journal *"Daedalus Hyperboreus"* where both a project for a flying machine "heavier than air" and the laws for transmission of thoughts between people could be presented. The King also would designate Emanuel Assessor in the country's very important College of Mines; however, it was a post of honor without pay for Emanuel. Many changes were brought on with the shooting of the King at Fredrikshald on 30 November 1718.

Something very important soon happened for Emanuel: The reigning Queen Ulrika Eleonora, sister of Charles XII, elevated Emanuel to noble status; *both* according to a rule for children in Bishop's families, and because of his status as Assessor of the College of Mines.

He now took the seat as head of the *Swedenborg* noble family in the Swedish Parliament Noble House, where he would be an active member for fifty years.

The coming years must have been economically and socially more secure for Emanuel. His own mother had died early; however, he must have been a real favorite of his stepmother, who was of the wealthy family Bergius, as he became her universal heir. As often is the case, there was a conflict with his other relatives concerning the inheritance, but settlements were made. He lived with his sister Hedwig and her husband Lars Bentzelstierna, who was also a colleague at the College of Mines, at Brunkebergstorg in Stockholm. After a short while, Swedenborg received a large apartment at Stora Nygatan 7 in Stockholm. There he also had a servant named Olof.

Swedenborg early on came to love the idea of "the kingdom of uses" and saw the clear connection between a coming prosperity and a technical and economic reform in the thinking of state and societies. King Charles had to the highest degree stimulated Swedenborg's thoughts concerning new methods of counting and calculating. Central topics were at the time the beginning of a demand on the declaration of all citizens' incomes and the use of possible objects of taxation during undeniably hard times. David Dunér in a brilliant dissertation noted that Emanuel Swedenborg, after the King's death, seems to have lost all interest for their common counting experiments. Swedenborg however did publish a strong appeal for the base of ten in all counting, especially pointing out a connection with taxation of the common citizen. However, 150 years would pass before the decimal system broke through in Sweden.

Swedenborg no doubt sought to faithfully fulfill his office at the important College of Mines. The work day was longer than now and leave on Saturdays was unthinkable. Swedenborg was also Inspector of Mines, which meant a lot of travel to his forefather's home country in Dalecarlia. He did not escape being concerned over the poor social conditions of the miners. Soon there were also periods of leave he used for studies in various parts of the European continent. His cousin received the property mentioned in Sveden as family inheritance, while Emanuel Swedenborg in return received Starbo at the lake Väsman near Ludvika in southern Dalecarlia. Some decades later he sold Starbo and bought a house and property at Hornsgatan in Stockholm, which soon became his permanent residence.

As he was performing his duties of office, Swedenborg continued his intense ambition to collect and summarize all available human knowledge and join the philosophical principles of the ancient sages with the most modern technology and all its inventions. The *Dream Diary* from the early 1740's reflects his energetic effort to conquer new domains of knowledge, and to seek to fathom the real dimensions of depth in human existence. He sought the structure of creation, made fundamental analyses of the human body and also the natural world. Everything seemed to correspond to something higher and in vivid pictures; he saw the wonderful interconnectedness of the whole cosmos, of all life, and all worlds. He was living in Stockholm, in an outer peaceful atmosphere of friends, neighbors, and a few servants.

Among these servants, he often hired a married couple, "the garden couple", to arrange the household when he did not want to be disturbed because of the intensity of his work. He did not eat full meals, but rather was content with having "simpler" buns, of wheat and coffee. At the same time, we know that he could frequent the better places in town such as the tavern Gyldene Freden (The Golden Peace) in the central town between the bridges.

In mathematical and geometric figures, he thought he could see something pointing to a transcendent world, "eternally true and independent of the human dimension" (David Dunér), which draws our attention to the Divine, to what is perfectly beautiful and divine. According to Swedenborg, all human functions and the human soul itself functioned as machines, but as machines with a higher life. Swedenborg dedicated himself with much labor during this early period to the task of proving to the human senses the immortality of the soul.

All natural phenomena to Swedenborg became echo temples and mirror halls, witnessing a deeper reality. The whole world appeared to speak a "hieroglyphic" language, through metaphors, correspondences, and analogies of sense. Swedenborg wrote the unfinished sketches in "a hieroglyphic key" whose symbolic world closely reminds us of the themes in the French poet Baudelaire's poem "Les Correspondences".

An important year for Swedenborg was 1734 when three large volumes of Swedenborg's "*Opera Philosophica et Mineralia*" were published in Leipzig, with the support of the Kurfurst, the local Prince. One volume was "*Principia*" on the principles of the creation of the world, and two mineralogical works on "*De Ferro*", "On Iron", and a third volume, "*De Cupro*", "On Copper". In these, we see among other things images and descriptions of fossils and descriptions of methods to best haul up the precious metals, especially the copper of the Falun Mine.

Swedenborg also visited Leipzig in 1734 and must have had many good contacts with people, interestingly also one of the other stipendees of the Kurfurst that year was Johann Sebastian Bach. As parliamentarian and member of the secret chamber (government) in Stockholm, he was able to inhibit a new war with Russia. In connection with this, he was accepted into the Russian Academy of Sciences in St. Petersburg.

David Dunér pointed out that in Bach's musical scores there is a metaphoric thinking, fully in the Spirit of Swedenborg, and "number mysticism, esoteric, secret signs". (p. 183)

No clear break with the earlier collaborator Christopher Polhem is known and no doubt Swedenborg followed closely the work of Polhem at the Slussen docks in Stockholm. When Polhem died in 1751 at almost ninety years of age, Swedenborg walked in his funeral train and was present at the funeral ceremony in the Maria Magdalena Church at Hornsgatan on the Southside of Stockholm. From the invisible world a relentless researcher asks Swedenborg to get permission to use his earthly sight and hearing, to be able to hear what the presiding priest is saying. What he heard was that he would sleep until the Last Day. He said he had had enough of that poor message. Swedenborg tells of this in his Spiritual Diary.

He had worked a lot with Polhem in his workshop at Stjärnsund in eastern Dalecarlia and probably met his daughter Emerentia there and also the person who was successor to the father, as the able leader of Stjärnsund, and with other colleagues.

Emanuel had gotten to know the sisters Maria and Emerentia well and also within the family received a promise to be able to marry the latter. Emerentia. He also came to know another of Polhem's entourage, Elisabet Stjerncrona, who later married Gyllenborg. The later contact remained after Gyllenborg's death, after which she seems to have come into a very close relationship with Emanuel Swedenborg. Polhems's daughters were soon out of the picture as possibly Swedenborg's future betrothed and he remained unmarried until his death. Also, now there was a cooler relationship between the families because the collaboration in work soon discontinued.

No doubt Swedenborg and Polhem met again in 1739 when they were welcomed by the President Carl von Linné and were being confirmed as members of the recently established Royal Academy of Science. He always wanted to be faithful to science. He collaborated in the Royal Academy Journal and later republished his earlier work on finding the longitude at sea and about the risks involved in the "depreciation and appreciation" of the Swedish currency.

In the work *Principia* he determines the first creation, the limit between the infinite and the finite, and the concept of the mathematical point. He joins with the philosopher Descartes' doctrines on the cosmos. The point has a Janus face that at the same time envisions the infinite, the totally indefinite, as well as looks to the incipient material creation.

With time Swedenborg found that the study of the geometric and mathematical laws was not sufficient to be able to penetrate the real depth of the dimensions of existence, nor to prove the spiritual nature of human beings and a life after the death of the material body. However, Swedenborg had deeply studied the human psyche and had in a wonderful way been able to localize the human psyche's activities to special areas of the brain (in his book titled, 'The Brain') whose information is still used to this day.

Swedenborg's notes in his Diary in the 1740's witnesses a severe crisis, filled with earthly temptations but also of a heavenly presence and of Divine revelation. He enters darkness and desperation concerning his results of research but is strengthened and liberated in his interior by very stiring visions of Christ and experiences of a calling to a higher mission. This was close to the usual age for pensioning. He asked for leave from College of Mines and this was granted.

The message of human immortality and the Divine mission behind all earthly images now comes to him as a revelation which he also confirmed by reason. By the power of revelation, he is now to experience how our small world bears witness of a higher and invisible world, a heavenly and Divine. He also was clear that the one and only eternal God had taken human form in Jesus Christ and that the writings are witness of this; that the Word is from the same God, and that it could be interpreted to have an inner meaning that is to be found beneath the very letter.

The source for this knowledge was foremost an intensive study of the Biblical writings themselves, also in the original languages and in the Latin translations. There are many unpublished manuscripts, often with commentary, that bear witness to this. It would also be rather impossible to deny that Swedenborg had taken lesson from the available traditions of learning.

In an article in the Encyclopedia *Nordisk Familjebok* in 1918, A. F. Åkerberg and Hjalmar Holmquist summarizes it as follows:
"A special place ought the late medieval Jewish mysticism, kabbala, and its furtherance by Pico della Mirandola have been for Swedenborg. From kabbala and (neo Platonism) he in 1740-42 received the most essential element, the theory of correspondence, that he developed in the manuscript *Clavis Hieroglyphica* (1741). According to this, every natural thing on the planet is a representative of spiritual things and affections, the animal, plant, and mineral realms, houses, food, clothing, the human face, speech and behavior, fog, rain, flashes, etc onward endlessly; oxen and steers correspond to the affections of the natural senses, sheep and lamb to the spiritual senses etc."

Martin Lamm and Inge Jonsson have in their studies shed further light on these sides of Swedenborg. In 1749 in London, Swedenborg published a large volume in Latin with the title *"Arcana Coelestia"*, "Heavenly Secrets", the first in a series of expositions of the First and Second Book of Moses, Genesis and Exodus, set out according to the allegorical and symbolic system of correspondences. For a large part, the Bible text is here seen as symbolic, for example the days of creation and ancient history. The seven days of creation, according to Swedenborg, tell about the human being converted from selfishness in the story of creation in seven steps. The story of the Patriarchs with Abraham longing for a son and the birth of the son after an angelic vision, told about the Divine Human of the Lord and his substantial entry into this world as Jesus Christ, the center which Swedenborg reveals even the most despicable stories in the Old Testament in the deepest sense were all about. The story of the sacrifice of Abraham's son would in the same way witness how the way of truth for human beings of this world could become a way of the cross, one of temptations, suffering and death, but also about resurrection and the way of new birth, the way of eternal hope. War and enemies are translated into our own inner enemies to avoid "contempt for others in comparison to ourselves" – a common expression with Swedenborg.

Without an inner examination in the deepest conjunction with reason and conscience the achievement of a deeper spirituality is impossible. In our worship of the Divine Christ, our senses present Divine Human and the origin of all human form; whereby, the Spirit of the Lord descends into us in the same measure as we want to do good, thus joining the descending love with wisdom. Swedenborg undeniably made a journey on an inner plane towards even more deeper insights. Thus, he felt an assurance of the life of the soul living in a substantial body after death and that a real, fully active human life, with new working tasks would await him after the death of the body.

In the beginning of the work *Arcana* Swedenborg explains: By "the Lord's Divine mercy it has been granted me now for some years to be constantly and uninterruptedly in company with spirits and angels, hearing them speak and in turn speaking with them. In this way it has been given me to hear and see wonderful things in the other life, which have never before come to the knowledge of any man, nor into his idea." (AC 5)

The risen and "glorified" Christ, the revelation of the only God, is in the centre of Swedenborg's religious vision, or that Christ is the "son of God" not the naturally human "son of Mary". In the beginning of the *Arcana* we find the following statement: "In the following work, by the name Lord is meant the Savior of the world, Jesus Christ, and Him only; and He is called "the Lord" without the addition of other names. Throughout the universal heaven, "He" it is who is acknowledged and adored as Lord, because "He" has all sovereign power in the heavens and on earth... In the universal heaven they know no other Father than the Lord..." (AC 14, 15)

All sacred scripture is thus witness, in its inner sense, to this one and only One and is written in "correspondences", yet this did not mean that they could be read and understood through some sort of code. An exterior understanding of correspondences would surely have been able to remove the intellectual barriers of most readers. However, according to Swedenborg, the true understanding could only come through the spirit of the Lord's inner light with a sincerely striving and seeking human being as explained in the *Arcana Coelestia*. Swedenborg was in the spiritual world and was witness to a "Last Judgment." At this time, all the heavens and hells in the other world were set in order, all according to each and everyone's inner ruling love, all reorganized according to the seriousness and depth of everyone's spiritual quest. The mystical experience, not the mathematical calculation, would now be the door to the true inner understanding of the spiritual depths.

In a similar way, one could now understand the fables and myths of other peoples and of the ancients which were written knowing the language of correspondences. Light and progress among humans would be able to continue but one could look forward to a new state of society descending from heaven, "the descending New Jerusalem".

Here the Lord's Divine Providence would forever lead us; but an end to history was not in sight. Our task would be to bravely and sincerely, take responsibility for ourselves and for our fellow human beings through a new education, and a new build up of our society for the welfare of all people, in preparation for a new reformation in the spiritual world, which all of us will enter some time.

The borderlines and separate denominations of religions will be toned down and eventually cease and instead a common human bond will enter upon the scene, regardless of doctrinal differences.

About this Swedenborg writes in *Arcana*: "In the Christian world it is doctrinal matters that distinguish churches; and from them men call themselves Roman Catholics, Lutherans, and Calvinists, or the Reformed and the Evangelical, and by other names. It is from what is doctrinal alone that they are so called; which would never be if they would make love to the Lord and charity toward the neighbor the principal of faith. Doctrinal matters would then be only varieties of opinion concerning the mysteries of faith, which truly Christian men would leave to everyone to hold in accordance with his conscience, and would say in their hearts that a man is truly a Christian when he lives as a Christian, that is, as the Lord teaches. Thus from all the differing churches there would be made one church; and all the dissensions that come forth from doctrine alone would vanish; yea, all hatreds of one against another would be dissipated in a moment, and the Lord's kingdom would come upon the earth." (AC 1799)

One has sometimes speculated over the connection between Swedenborg's symbolic Bible interpretation and the one common in European Freemasonry, where there are striking mutual similarities. Significant for the Swedish Masonic Orders were the brothers Samuel (1688-1743) and Mårten Trierwald (1691-1747), both at times friends of Swedenborg and at the same time representing a Christian humanism with connections to the thinking of the ancients, which would have agreed with Swedenborg's thinking.

Mårten Trierwald and Emanuel Swedenborg are usually mentioned as having been impressed by ideas from England of introducing the steam-engine in Sweden.

Without a doubt one could point to certain words and concepts in *Arcana,* which in their spiritual symbolism could be seen as keys for an understanding of the allegories here; however, an interpretation of Bible texts or other texts with the help of technical codes is never the case. Instead, all deeper understanding of the Biblical texts and of Swedenborg's later works, "the thirty volumes" as they are called in

20

the English-speaking world, depend, according to Swedenborg, on the person's spiritual state and on the degree of enlightenment from the Lord he or she receives.

We live, according to Swedenborg, in a symbiosis, in a commonality of thought with angels and spirits in the other world, so that our understanding agrees with that of the angels by our side. It is said in *Arcana* that the angels understand the Word best when small children read it, who are in a state of innocence and have not yet let their self-love formulate any false interpretations. (AC 1776). These words here indicate that there are many barriers to our inner light, to true enlightenment that have to be removed before we can begin to clearly see the inner sense.

In works after 1749, Swedenborg chose to explain word for word and comment upon some of the biblical writings that to many appear most difficult and opaque, for example, the First and Second Book of Moses (Genesis and Exodus) and the Book of Revelations. Both the literal truth of the days of creation and the authorship of Moses to the subject books had begun to be questioned. Certain occurrences and actions in the books, among the "chosen" people, could also be strongly questioned from an ethical perspective. But the literal sense these still signifies important spiritual events that actually happened in the world, such as the descent of the son of God, and how God's Human nature delivered mankind from the slavery of selfishness and tells how our road to the community of angels and heavenly beatitude comes only through many trials, both here in this world and through trials in the passage to the other world.

This is the message in the Book of Revelations whose wars and natural catastrophes are a representation of our struggles on an inner plane. In the final vision is shown how New Jerusalem descends and is a new Kingdom of God, and the resurrection of the dead becomes a reality.

We must, each of us, examine ourselves for great spiritual revolu-

tions to occur. The stories in the Word are never predicting external happenings such as some sudden punishment or a destruction
of earthly societies or dwellings, this will not be the case. An end to
human existence is not what is being talked about, it is not the meaning; our earthly existence will, as before, forever function as a "seed-
bed for heaven". (Swedenborg in the work *On the Last Judgment*.)

This new message from Swedenborg, about God's eternal kingdom in
the heavens, being as well here as on earth; and that His arrival is being
explained to be a progressing new understanding of the Divine truth
- early on this is what began to fascinate readers of the Writings.

The whole spiritual world is described in works from 1758, published in London, "according to what has been heard and seen". Every human soul through the mercy of the Lord goes there after the
death of the body in this world, and goes to a place that is according
to the ruling love of each and everyone. There is a description of Af-
ricans immediately becoming angels because of their pure and simple
worship of God, and also how those who have loved each other in
this world can become happy couples in the next. No one is forced;
instead there is the deepest Divine respect for each and everyone's
freedom and reason.

During his later years, Emanuel Swedenborg had to spend a lot of energy to support his friends Gabriel Beyer and Johan Rosén, both lecturers at the Gymnasium school in Gothenburg; where the youth are
prepared for a priestly profession. A collection of sermons by Beyer
written in Swedenborg's spirit had been approved. However, as in
some sense justified, complaints against the decision of the Church's
authority had been begun to flow in. One complaint, unexpectedly
questioned these two lecturers right to teach. It became a drawn out
judicial case with demands from various places. In the meanwhile, Swedenborg died, first before them, then Rosén died, and then Beyer died.
However, Swedenborg did write powerful defenses for his friends.

In 1770, Swedenborg went to Holland to publish his last large and summarizing work, "*True Christian Religion*", and after a short visit there; he went to spend his last days in England, and that is where he finished his earthly existence on 29 March 1772.

During his last days, he was connected to a physician and fellow believer by the name of Husband Messiter, who stood near him during his last moments in London in the artisan Shearsmith's house.

Messiter represented a circle of free minded men of Jewish faith from which one member, Gumpertz Levison, in close contact with Swedenborg's friends, would contribute to the freedom of Jews to practice their religion in Sweden. Also, cooperation with the Jewish tradition was already present in the circle of Benzelius in Uppsala, to which Swedenborg belonged, and who saw that the former rabbi Johan Kemper was hired at the university teaching the kabbalist *Zohar*. Apparently, Kemper belonged to the Jewish humanism that tried to build bridges between religions, in contrast to the strong faith in the literal sense that otherwise was characteristic of the Jewish groups at this time.

According to Swedenborg, the true human world was so constituted that each and everyone in his designated place took responsibility and did his duty, not only towards the private human being, but also towards the society that was closest at hand. But our love must also encompass all people in all of the societies in the world, and not least in all religions without demanding these to convert and become like us.

"Now it is permitted to with the intellect enter the mysteries of faith" (*True Christian Religion* 508). This Swedenborg saw written above the door to a temple in the spiritual world.

Now heavenly light can flow into the beliefs of the faith of all human beings, and in the same measure by free will he or she can turn around to follow the higher truth.

Then an inner sight of belief will follow where all representative forms in the worlds will mirror a Divine Spiritual influx.

Swedenborg, and his Mission as Revelator of New Truths

Olle Hjern

The decisive moment in Emanuel Swedenborg's life took place in the Hague in 1744, between the 6th and 7th of April, when he had a vision of the face of Jesus. The vision was so undeniable and compelling that Swedenborg discontinued the greater part of his scientific work and turned himself over to being the mediator of a message to all humanity, received directly from the Lord Jesus Christ.

Swedenborg relates that he saw the face of Jesus Christ in a vision, and experienced His presence and tells that in this vision he was given a mission from God. The mission was to reveal the truths of an interior meaning to the Bible and restore the truths that had been lost to Christianity.

Swedenborg thus rejected the belief that God was three separate persons (the Father, the Son, and the Holy Spirit). This doctrine and the belief in three persons in God Swedenborg totally discarded. He came to see that the only true God was the Lord Jesus Christ who is Jehovah in the Old Testament.

When the Bible mentions Father, Son, and the Holy Spirit, what is meant are different aspects and representations of the one God.
The Father symbolizes the Divine Itself and is the soul of Jesus. The Son, is His human nature which became the Divine Human, The Holy Spirit is His Holy Proceeding; the Divine power that emanates from him.

Swedenborg also came to acknowledge that the doctrine of atonement is not possible according to this view of God. God became man to fight down the powers of Hell that threatened the freedom of mankind. On the question of justification, the New Church teaches that if a person doesn't turn towards God and live a righteous life, then they are not justified by the death of Christ. A belief in the Lord Jesus Christ as the only true God, is essential. Swedenborg explains how the doctrine of faith alone is misinterpreted and misunderstood and should be rejected.

Instead, what is necessary, is doing what is good, with actual human deeds, and loving God. This is what is decisive in every person's salvation.

A new view of the Bible is founded on the truths of Swedenborg's doctrine that proclaims that Scripture has an inner, spiritual meaning that is hidden by the letter's literal sense. Swedenborg's mission from God is to reveal the inner meaning of the Bible to humanity and show that it has been written in the ancient language of correspondences.

An example is in the book of Revelations 19:11-16, where it tells of a rider on a white horse in the sky, who is followed by riding hosts of angels. According to Swedenborg's language of correspondences this story means that the Lord Himself shall come to us with a true understanding of the Word of God. Each detail of the story has a certain symbolic meaning.

The host of angels on white horses correspond to innumerable heavenly truths. A horse symbolizes a spiritual understanding, especially here, the horse is meaning an understanding of God's Word. Just as the horse carries the rider to the end of the journey, so our understanding of God's Word carries us forward on the road leading to Heaven

According to Swedenborg, there are certain books that make up the Bible that have an internal series that interiorly relate to the Lord's Glorification. However, some of the books of the Bible do not have this continuous internal series within the stories and therefore are not considered to be Divinely inspired in the same way, but are only Apocrypha. In the New Testament it is the Gospels and the Book of Revelations that have a connecting internal seance with full validity.

Swedenborg explains how the second coming of Christ and the Last Judgment has actually already happened and he tells exactly how it took place in the spiritual world in 1757. He writes that he was a witness to how a New Heaven was established and how it is described by correspondences in the book of Revelation. When John saw in a vision in *Revelation* 21, Swedenborg explains how this represented the New Church descending to earth. This New Church is to be called The New Jerusalem and will have a new understanding of the Divine and as it descends, it will be a Crown to all churches.

When Jesus spoke of coming again, 'coming in the skies', this was not meant to be taken literally. It was never to be interpreted literally, instead the skies signify the Letter of the Word. It is by means of these new truths that the Lord God Jesus Christ will scatter the false tenets of belief that are based on obscure, misunderstood passages in the Bible. These amazing new truths will explain the sense of the Letter of the Word and give spiritual light to those who seek it. These truths will open mankind to a new understanding of the Divine and be the foundation of a new spiritual understanding.

Life after death in the spiritual world takes a prominent place in Swedenborg's Writings. The truths of the New Church teach that the body that is laid in the grave will never more be needed and not resurrected, as is taught in the "old church" – the decaying Christianity.

After three days a person is resurrected into the spiritual world where they are met by near and dear family and friends, and by angels. Spiritual beings are all people who have lived in the natural world. 'Angels' that have not been humans do not exist.

The person resurrected does not immediately come into heaven or hell. At first they will be in the world of spirits where they will learn about themselves. This state is where their interior loves can be revealed to them and where they learn how they will fit into their future life there. Where a person chooses to live is according to their sense of what is good and true or false and evil. God does not condemn anyone. When a person only loves himself, and chooses to love what is evil, he condemns himself. Swedenborg explains that the spiritual world is so reminiscent of this existence that sometimes people do not at first notice that they are dead and have left the material body.

The "gates" to heaven and hell stand open to all. Everyone is drawn to where he or she feels at home. In heaven, angels are a representative of their ruling love and understanding of the truths that correspond to their piety and spiritual development. They are in the happiness of their life and are concerned with acts of love such as the use of the education of children that have died at early age. There are a host of activities in heaven, just as in this world, and angels there are constantly learning new things and developing in goodness and truth. To grow old in heaven is the same as rejuvenating. The angels have the same gender there as they have here on earth. They also marry and those who have been harmoniously married on earth continue to be married in heaven. Hell has also various divisions where the bad will settle according to their inner ruling love. They continue in their life, just as they were in this earth, to love to steal, to lie, to blaspheme, or to try to murder etc. Everything in our earthly world mirrors that which is in a higher world. There is a relationship, a "correspondence", between the worlds.

The last work that Swedenborg completed was "*True Christian Religion*", published in Amsterdam in 1771. Towards the end of his life he received the Last Supper by the pastor in the Swedish Church in London, Arvid Ferelius, who asked him to recall his doctrines, and asked if he was sure about their being the truth. Swedenborg answered him: "As truly as you see myself before your eyes, so true also is everything I have written, and I could have said more if it had been permitted to me."

Swedenborg was once asked, how from a philosopher he became a theologian? He answered, "In the same way, fishermen became the Lord's followers and apostles". Swedenborg explained that, "from his youth, he had been a spiritual fisherman, that is, one who searches, "a person who investigates and teaches natural truths and afterwards spiritual truths rationally". Swedenborg here emphasizes that a person who does not want to thoroughly explore natural truths, isn't likely to explore spiritual truths. Without a will to explore what is purely natural, no one will become a prophet of the Lord who will be able to teach Divine truths.

"Now explain what your teaching is all about", followed the next question to Swedenborg. He replied: "These are its two principles of it":

"That God is one and that there is a conjunction between charity and faith".

"These things are denied by the theology that is taught today".
(*The Intercourse between Soul and Body*, 20)

Answers concerning Swedenborg's Life

The Revelator of Secrets of the Word and a Spiritual Guide

Olle Hjern

Swedenborg was born in Stockholm on the 29th of January 1688. The family came from Dalecarlia and was involved in mining for generations. The father, Jesper Svedberg, had become a military pastor and court preacher in Stockholm. Near Falun there is still the mining household that belonged to the family Svedberg and where later, ennobled members of the family took the name Swedenborg in 1719.

Swedenborg was only 11 years old when he arrived at Uppsala University, where at the time students and university teachers frequently were employed as "informators", as were the young boys that often arrived there. These young boys later on began to follow the Professor's lectures at the University. Swedenborg, still Svedberg, took part eagerly in the academic teaching in Uppsata, among other things he must have taken the opportunity to study ancient languages, as well as ancient and more modern philosophy. He acquired great skill in composing Latin verse – something that was taught at the University. In 1709, he "disputed" in Latin, and defended a text of maxims by Seneca and Publilius Syrus.

Next followed a period in England, with studies in natural sciences and technology. After his return to Sweden, he soon became involved in Christopher Polhem's technical company. At one time he was Polhem's assistant in the mechanical shop in Stjärnsund in Dalecarlia.

With support of the Swedish king, Charles XII, Swedenborg and Polhem published the journal "Daedalus Hyperboreus", where much technology was presented; for example, Swedenborg sketched a design for a flying machine. The King, as much as possible, tried to engage both these men as military engineers. His attempts, in respect to Emanuel, were in connection with the war in Norway. Apparently this resulted in a break between them shortly before the death of the king.

In 1718, the Swedish form of government was monarchical rule, but after Charles XII perished, this soon started to change. Instead the power of four estates (nobles, priests, citizens, and peasants) was introduced, For example, the four estates of the Parlement took over most of the previous royal power. This step was apparently very much liked by Swedenborg, because with his ennoblement in 1719 he received a seat and a say in the House of Nobles as head of his noble family. During his whole life he remained active in the Parlement and came to be especially interested in economical issues. He was in many ways, as much as possible, a friend of "mercantilism", i.e. the development and production of the land. He often warned against a return to monarchical rule.

Swedenborg plainly supported the societies of the arts, letters and science, and was well familiar with the rich mythological symbolism and embellishment of both the Baroque and the Rococo. Much of this was to serve as a background pattern for both his early and later his works. Certainly, Swedenborg would have have delighted in the progress of science of today, as well as reminding us of many older inventions that could now be applied and developed. He wanted to combine "The Wisdom of the Ancients" with the newest research discoveries. In any case, he believed in the spiritual and ethical values of ancient sages as necessary for the training of contemporary scientists.

Swedenborg became a mining engineer, Assessor in the College of Mines, and during his whole life, until his sixties, he was a very respected citizen in the country. He was always kind and did his duties, however at times he did appear somewhat shy and withdrawn. During the last decades of prophetic activity, he had many friends, but some people became reluctant to continue the friendship and some even became hostile because of his behavior. It is said that efforts were made to have him interned in a mental institution. Most people emphasized his good character and pleasant manners. It was only when discussion reached religion and the spiritual world did he became strange many claimed.

In 1749, there was published anonymously in London the first huge volume of his work "Arcana Coelestia", "Heavenly Secrets", which was an allegorical exposition word by word of Genesis, at the same time having a series of purely narrative passages, often passages about life after death and about the spiritual world. It was ten years later that it became clear to all people that the Swede, Emanuel Swedenborg, was the author of this work; where he presented a new theology, and a wholly new view of both the material and the spiritual world. This view he presented to the world as being commissioned from on high, he explained that God himself had called, enlightened and inspired him.

In many ways it deviated from the contemporary Christianity, but clearly represented both a Biblical and Christian tradition. In the center of Swedenborg's theology is the doctrine of One God, who embodies principles of Wisdom and Love, Truth and Good, and in this world is revealed as the resurrected, the "glorified" or divinized Jesus Christ, who is Father, Son and Holy Spirit in one Divine Human. He thus incarnated the highest values, those which through time had been mediated to humanity through prophets and wise people.

Through their attitude towards the highest values, human beings chose, according to Swedenborg his or her place spiritually, the place in the spiritual and invisible world surrounding us all.
"Faith alone" in a Protestant sense, or a purely exterior recognition of confessions of faith, means nothing for the spiritual awakening and development of a human being. According to Swedenborg, instead,

what is important is the degree to which one lets the truth that one has recognized as true become active in one's life, with charity and a love of humanity. This holds true in all religions of the world which Swedenborg sees are all various paths to the same God.

The spiritual world is according to Swedenborg, a world of uses, just as the earthly human world ought to be. The natural and spiritual worlds correspond to each other. Swedenborg explains how this natural world is a reflection of a higher spiritual one and that in the coming life, there are societies and also work to be done and normal outer surroundings for the people there, which is an analogy with our existence here.

Swedenborg has often inspired people with thoughts of societal reform, even revolutionaries and also rather extreme Utopians. All his life he was engaged in social questions but worked within the frame of the 'Age of Freedom', Parliamentary system. When he was older he wrote special religious messages about the doctrine of the "New Church" that were in contrast to many religious movements of the time. These writings were friendly to Society because they emphasized that the most pious acts were to make an effort to help Society, rather than to going to Church and dedicating oneself to only a pious exercise. Swedenborg held Society to be our neighbor just as much as a single individual, and wrote that the "New Church" would include thoughts about a more just and better society, this he said, can be seen as something self evident. But Swedenborg never came forward with any political program and therefore reformists of both "right and "left" have been able to seek support from him.

To be useful to the common good, as well as practicing purity of mind and willingly following God's word and keeping a good order in society are mentioned in his rules for life. They are taken from a report of a speech by Sandels in Stockholm after Swedenborg's death – there is no written original.

Swedenborg explicitly explained how after long preparation, he had received enlightenment from the Lord. He was very well educated in natural things, and he obviously was spiritually enlightened. He stressed that reason was the foundation of the revelation he had received from the Lord and that he was to mediate this revelation to human kind. In the beginning of these spiritual revelations Swedenborg told of several visions of Christ, who in one instance declared to Swedenborg that He was the One God of heaven and earth. However, Swedenborg never founded a special Church society. Surely, he must have wanted, at least theoretically to give the established churches the chance to receive his "from the Lord" mediated doctrine.

In his authorized religious writings there are rather detailed prescriptions for baptism and other rituals that could, in the long run, not but help bring on the establishment of new church societies, even if one did not make a reform in complete accord with Swedenborg's prescriptions. In many ways "New Church" doctrine is closer to the Catholic than the Protestant churches, but the thought of the Spirit of God as directly inherent in the Church, or of some papal primacy, must have been totally alien to Swedenborg.

The early twentieth century Archbishops Ekman and Söderblom did speak very positively of Swedenborg and not entirely without understanding. Right now the respect for Swedenborg's importance for our cultural inheritance ought to be a positive factor. Popes and archbishops probably do not know much about Swedenborg. Their judgments would be dependent on others. A benign concern has in later years been noticed among Polish Catholics - perhaps this has moved the Pope in the same direction (Johannes Paulus II).

Swedenborg was the last to deny that prayer and spiritual practices in various forms could mean a lot to human inner reformation, at the same time, he warned of a one sided cultivation of pure "spirituality,"- of prayer, meditation and holy services. Certainly he would approve of all of these practices if they did not encourage a social withdrawal from the world with its duties and assignments.

Swedenborg himself, was never a hermit, and even if for long periods of time lived rather ascetically, he never promoted living a restricted life of that sort as of any value. He was never married, but never gave any reason for the cause thereof. He was often critical of monkish establishments and life in the cloisters, but clearly had a sense for the cultural contribution that often has been made and was done within the walls of the monasteries.

Swedenborg was undoubtedly an optimist concerning people's possibilities to "as of of oneself" to realize a heavenly life and order here in this world. But he also had a clear sense of how slowly and sluggishly people take on new thoughts and new truths. Therefore he foresaw a longer "desert state of vastation" for the New Church. At the same time, he predicted times of more spiritual freedom and enlightenment than in the past. But on the whole he did not want to say anything of the future. It isn't good and useful for humans to know the future he claimed.

Everything in our spiritual development is dependent on the church developing reason through continuously taking responsibility and seriously planning a path in life. We must have a feeling that we ourselves can with free choice and contributions, shape our own future and in that way be a co-creator to God and caretaker of the world.

Swedenborg was very tolerant of all other religions and saw them as different paths to God and their traditions as possible remains of an ancient original revelation. At the same time, he always underlined that the full revelation of God was within the sphere of the Bible and Christianity.

Swedenborg's thoughts on other nations is perhaps not entirely easy to grasp. But first of all he saw humanity as a unity, as a reflection of the "Grand Human" of heaven seeing that all people had an important and special spiritual inheritance that they should cultivate if it was good, and flee from and change if it was bad.

The New Church has organized societies in a many countries. The largest i in England, United States, Canada, South African Republic, Lesotho, Ghana and Nigeria. Smaller groups are spread in various locations in Scandinavia, on the European continent and in East Asian countries, India, Burma, Korea, Japan and the Philippines.

Some regard Swedenborg as saintly – "he lived like a philosopher" declared one his first followers. One can surmise that without a large degree of spiritual regeneration the enlightenment and revelation could not have been given to him. Swedenborg's own precepts or those of Church societies is that Jesus Christ was both the revealed God and an example for us to follow in life. Emanuel Swedenborg understood this clearly.

He would certainly had had a lot to preach and to perform if he had lived today, especially concerning a religion based on reason, a reasonable Christianity that at the same time would take responsibility and care of the whole spiritual inheritance of humanity.

It can also be said that he saw himself especially elected by Providence during a time of spiritual change, when old orthodoxies and old spiritual tyrannies were breaking down and new ways needed to be searched to preserve the spiritual inheritance of humanity.

It is true that when religion is present in what is new in an understandable language it can florish. Certainly, Swedenborg's influence in time grew in his own native country, but church injunctions and all sorts of prejudices have undoubtedly hindered spiritual movements. At the same time, Sweden has a very distinguished literary Swedenborg tradition, with authors such as

Thorild, Almqvist, Strindberg, Ekelund and many others. His influence continues even if it often happens in a fragmentary way.

The human being's greatest dangers in our time would, according to Swedenborg have been that people did not take responsibility; that churches, societal orders, nature and culture were misused and man became destructive instead of preserving and building up society. Swedenborg would surely have had thoughts on the possibility that we human beings can destroy the whole earth, but still, according to Swedenborg, we can make it into a paradise, and during all circumstances humanity would live on, like "a seed-bed for heaven".

Swedenborg is the revelator of the secrets of the Word and the spiritual guide who shows us that each of us must use our reason and seek for ourselves to acquire an enlightened reason, rather than blindly following.

A Spiritual Path

Olle Hjern

"Every truth is a mirror of the infinite"

Some year ago, a friend of mine in Stockholm, Pierre Stahre, asked me to do an interview about how I came to be interested in Emanuel Swedenborg. He was also inquiring about some of the main points and basic facts about Swedenborg. Perhaps Pierre Stahre thought of this as being preparatory work for making a film, because he had already had several successful short films that were shown on Swedish television and he might have expected this also to be presented on massmedia.

I received a series of detailed questions from him that were later compiled into a talk and then produced. It was recorded on tape and later written out. What was produced in that talk can be read here. It was published on the advice of Anders Hallengren, my assistant editor for Världarnas möte – Nya Kyrkans tidning (*The Meeting of Worlds - New Church Journal*). Certain autobiographic memoirs have been added.

My journey began in 1938

I probably first heard of Swedenborg in connection with the Jubilee of 1938 - as there was much being written about the man in the newspapers at the time, and also new stamps of him were being made. I also heard a dramatic play on the radio by Karl-Gustaf Hildebrand that same year, which made an especially strong impression on me. I do not remember clearly when this was but I also heard a lecture on the radio about Swedenborg by Tor Andreae. In any case, what he wrote on Swedenborg in books and essays and in *Den gamla prästgården* (*The Old Priestly Manor*) had a strong effect on me. Also my main teacher in Swedish in the gymnasium school was Åke Lagerholm. He had a benevolent attitude towards Swedenborg and a real dedication to Christian Platonism, which can be found in the authors of *Psalms and Poems*, Johan Olof Wallin and Esaias Tegnér.

Both in middle school and in the Gymnasium we were constantly reminded of the "son of the town" in Jönköping, who was Viktor Rydberg. In his Christian idealism and humanism one can find parallels to Swedenborg's religious views. Religion was clearly valued among the towns people, even if the extent of this religious spirit was harder to measure than in the more outwardly visible Pietist and Pentecostal groups.

In my hometown of Jönköping there was a lively interest and much activity in the Swedenborgian societies. I soon got to know the members there and many other people my parents knew. My father did not doubt that this lively sphere was related to a "Swedenborgian attitude". It is clear that my father's parents, who had lived in the region of Skara, had been in close contact with the so called "Skara Swedenborgianism" and were central figures within the "New Church" there. Also during the 1800's they had taken part in the education of the children that we are descended from.

In 1809, the New Church central figure Leonard Gyllenhaal, of Höberg manor, is noted as the patron to one of those I descended from. His father had fought in the war in Norway in 1718 and then had died. Some of my ancestors during the 1700's were part of the congregation that must have listened to Pastor Jonas Odhner's "Swedenborgian" preaching in the Varnhem Church. He worked there with the translation of Swedenborg's *True Christian Religion*, that was later published in Copenhagen.

My grandfather on my mother's side, was a schoolteacher and preacher and must have also had contacts with the New Church as he let a wellknown New Church man cooperate in his *Journal for Temperance*. Early on he was taken with an interest in the 'Waldenström Movement of Awakening' and formed a free Church society in Östrogötland. Later he was to end up in Missionsförbundet (the

Swedish Missionary Union). Parts of my mother's greater family were engaged in the so called "Irvingian" or Catholic Apostolic Free Church. Among them was the last priests to work in the sanctuary at Odengatan-Birger Jarlsgatan in Stockholm. It is now a central church for the Greek Orthodox.

The Period before the Second World War was a ferment of ideologies in Sweden. A large parts of the Swedish and European youth were fascinated by all sorts of utopias and dreams for the future, both political and religious. Nationalism and internationalism were present in movements for physical health, social repair and a return to nature; all were common "youth movements". These movements were of all different sorts and all showed great vitality. They promoted culture and education, but at the same time many could see them as tools for power thirsty leaders to use in a manipulative way to approach and then control the youth. Spiritual leaders of past times were often evoked and their words could certainly be misused, but thankfully were thus not forgotten. This was also the case with Emanuel Swedenborg, whose writings were used as discussion points in certain ideally oriented youth circles. This I had already heard of during my time in Middle School in Jönköping.

My teacher for Confirmation in the Swedish Church, Olle Helander, (I was then a member of it), introduced us confirmees into the then strong Oxford Movement in both its practice and thought (later Moral Rearmament). Now and then my contacts were renewed with this movement, whose pedagogy for meditation and its aim towards practical Christianity and religion in action, was strongly attractive to me. It resulted in a rather remarkable religious ecumenism. That many in the New Church saw parallels with their own tradition of thought is fully understandable.

This also sheds light on the New Church pastor Gustaf Bäckström's book *Världsväckelse* (*World Awakening*) for example, which I took an early interest in at about the same time as my first studies of Swedenborg's works began. I had a renewed contact with Olle Helander later on; he had become an interested reader of Swedenborg and had written essays (one published in *Svensk Teologisk kvartalstidskrift*) which shed light on August Strindberg's relation to Emanuel Swedenborg's writings.

Gymnasium School Influences

During my time in the Gymnasium school my religious interests were strenghtened to the highest degree because I was in a class where most of the students were active in Christian circles. After a period of time when I had become quite involved in the ancient Norse Traditions my interest began to shift more and more towards a Christian direction. One day we gymnasium friends went to a discussion concerning "Christianity and Humanism", arranged by ABF (The Workers Education Society) and one of the speakers, was the then very well known principal Gunnar Hirdman, defender of a "non-Christian Humanism".

The first opponent was a rather young pastor in the town, Erik Sandström, who I had heard of as a representative of the "Swedenborgians". He made a good impression on me and I was sympathetic to his arguements which seemed reasonable and appeared to take the edge off the anti-Christian arguments. This was in the beginning of the 1940's, and later during this decade I was to take part in his religious services. These were very important for my development. In between these later events was a period of engagement in Lutheran Pietism, formed by C. O. Rosenius and by the Norwegian theologian Olle Hallesby, who had many admirors among the Gymnasium students in Jönköping.

The Pastor Blomquist gathered us in "Kompletorier" and during meetings and conversation with the priest Bo Giertz, in Torpa, there were discussions with a charged atmosphere. Sometimes we listened to the young Olov Hartman and sometimes to the slightly older David Hedegård. The latter would center his discussion on the Bible but with a rather "Pentecostal" direction, which influenced me strongly, and surely was not without importance for me. Before the end of my time in the Gymnsium school I became a member of the Pentecostal congregation in Jönköping. The religious atmosphere was no doubt intense. The Gymnasium students gathered before the school morning prayer at 8 am and also gathered for private spiritual prayer sessions at 7 am.

My first meeting with the Pentecostal message was the author Sven Lindman, a remarkable preacher, who I later learned had benevolence towards the New Church. Shortly after my Student exam, I participated in a course with "Helgelseförbundet" (The Union of Sanctity), in the prophetical school in Götabro in Närke. This also strengthened my interest in the writings of Christian mysticism, together with the Bible,

Thomas a Kempis' *Om Kristi efterföljelse* (*On following Christ*), is a handbook of Godly devotion which I still have, and now and then pick up and read. I was a steady follower of its message for years. At the same time I became more and more into a life of prayer with strong inner experiences. God seemed to become as real as people around me. Sometimes I stepped forward publically as speaker in Pentecostal Churches in Jönköping, in Malmö, Lund and in Stockholm. A wonderful contact in Malmö was with the music leader Göte Strandsjö, who later, came to partcipate in our Ryno Sigstedt's New Church resurrection celebration.

In my immature youth, I was often dejected by the quarrels among both Pentecostals and Church Christians, to whom adherence to the Bible did not seem to help; sometimes Bible reading seemed to enhance the quarrels and oppositions. In this situation, I found in my father's library a small work by one of his friends who was a devoted Pasadena theosopher. He, himself was both a teacher and artist, even for a time with the later very famous artist John Bauer as pupil. The booklet was entitled *Vägen till frid, Dig hägnad* (*The Road to Peace, Dedicated to You*) and was foremost an exposition of the Buddhist eightfold path – "right speech", "right striving", "right thinking" etc, yet to some extent clothed in a Biblical Christian language. I could not reject this as false spirituality, I thought, rather that one would need this quiet and meditative religiousity as a permanent correction in the strife of practising real Christianity! I had also by then read Hellen Keller's *My Religion*, a summary exposition of Swedenborg and New Church doctrine that I highly appeciate. Of course it made an strong impression on me, but as I understood it at that time, it was too "literal" and "humanistic", thus it was not answering my need for a radical conversion or supported my belief in the letter. My need for an "awakening" and also"fundamentalism" was perhaps expressing a need for security in my existence.

During my Gymnasiusm years, I had also been fascinated by Nathan Söderblom's *Den Levande Guden* (*The Living God*) whose effort was to show that God has spoken through spiritual geniuses from many different directions and to a variety of world religions. The experience of this work I will never forget; but apparently it did not work as medicine against the more narrow minded Christianity I had begun to slide into.

Connecting to Swedenborg again

Soon, however, I met Pastor Jack Hårdstedt, a former marine officer, who during the war had led a missionary in Port Said, in Egypt, which had a connection to Stockholm, that I had hoped to join. Hårdstedt was later appointed editor in chief of the newspaper, Dagen, in Stockholm. During his time in Egypt he had become a dedicated follower of Swedenborg's doctrines and had great enthusiasm for his writings - which not being new to me caused me to rush to the library right after our meetings to borrow Swedenborg's works. This was possible in the places where I then resided, Jönköping and Lund.

A missionary in the ordinary sense I was not, but opportunities to preach to African societies I was not going to lack in the future. Soon after my first aquaintance with Swedenborg it was clear to me that the common views that were held among old friends of my previous missionary activity, were completely untenable. I rejected the idea that only Christian salvation could save believers of differing faiths or non-believing people from the literal fires of hell with its eternal torture. I came to the conclusion that what is important in a relationship with people of other cultures and religions, should be a dialogue showing respect for their differences and especially not trying to scare them into Christian conversion.

Opportunities for religious dialogue

Opportunities for religious dialogue with muslims was also frequent in the years to come, both in Sweden and in other countries. Something developed much differently than I first had imagined. I had previously imagined dialogue would only be directed towards conversions to Christian faith. At our first personal meeting, which took place in Tranås, Jack Hårdstedt told me much about his conversations with Copts and muslims in Egypt. The question was about God's unity and trinity and the whole problem about Christian Trinity apparently was a large part of the concern of spiritually seeking people. As they experienced the Western Christian message it could not give them satisfying answers in this. While wrestling with these problems, Swedenborg's *True Christian Religion* fell into Jack Hårdstedt's hands. There he finally found a clear and a human sense understandable presentation of the Christian Trinity! I was visiting in Stockholm shortly after this and took the opportunity to listen to the pastors Eric von Born and Gustaf Bäckström, who were both eager writers and each contributed with their own special aspects of the New Church message. Soon, to me personally, the psalm "Led milda ljus..." (Lead Kindly Light...) became a formulation of prayer to which I constantly returned.

Immediately after my Student exam in 1945, I arrived in the University town of Lund where I began to study history and at the same time I frequently participated in the meetings of three different Christian student organiszations. There I was confronted with Ole Hallesby, returned from the German concentration camp -

now a Professor at Oslo. He had been invited by the "Evangelicals".
Hallesby's writings I had read before, however his powerful Biblical
messages both impressed me and yet caused hesitation.

Certainly my contacts with friends in this context contributed
to improving my spiritual orientation, and to a reorientation and re-
newal. I came to a clearer insight that true Christianity was not to
escape this world, but was to actively live in it and take interest in the
life of culture and society. A special aid in this regard was the community in "Fria Kristliga Studentförbundet" (Free Christian Student
Union), which was a meeting place for foremost Free Church Students, on whose Board I had belonged for a while. There were some
especially important friendly contacts there that I remember. Among
whom were Berndt Gustafsson, Gunnar Hillerdal and Gunnar Fur.
A colourful member of the student circle was also Inga Andersson.
She was unconventional in her religious interests and standpoints.
Quite independently of me she sought out the New Church, after
which we soon were to start a family together.

Innermost consciousness of One God

Our teacher in literature at the Gymnasium school in Jönköping
had given us some of Esaias Tegnér's thoughts on 'satisficatio vicaria':
that God's Son had taken on sin in our place and had carried the punishment for all human sins - believing that the innoscent Son had
atoned the Father's wrath so that we could be forgiven. This doctrine,
the official one in the then present State Church, was characterized
as "a slaughter idea, blasphemous to both God and Reason" by Tegnér in letters dated 21 January 1821, written to his fellow Eric Gustaf
Geijer. These words we learned by heart, but neither the old C. O.
Rosenius nor the contemporary Pentecostal preachers could lure us
back to those beliefs. These doctrines had, in the deepest sense, become blasphemus to us because within one's innermost consciousness
it created an idea of two gods.

FKS offered contact with good preachers in the Swedish Missionary Society, among whom there were alternative views with emphasis on God's Love and God's unity and living according to the good tradition from the founders Ekman and Waldenström.

After a crisis and spiritual turn around, I seemed to able to see the doctrine of Christ's atonement in a clearer light, and thereby the road opened for a total acceptance of Emanuel Swedenborg's view.

A special Lunda group was formed among the students who had joined Pentacostal circles, and debates were intense about the crises and problems within this movement. Criticism of opinions in the movement could be harsh, but regardless of this we often particpated actively in the discussions. For example, we went for visits to hear the preaching in the congregations in Malmö. From this circle, I remember especially well my friends Sara and Harald Wollstad, Torsten Bergsten and Bo Strömstedt. None of us remained for long members of any Pentecostal Society. This circle with its various extensions and branches is described in Harald Wollstad's little book *Lundensiskt 40-tal* (The 40's in Lund).

Through the Christian Student Movement, I was able to make some journeys to Germany, both to the occupied Germany and to the divided Berlin. In place after place, I took part in conversations and debates with German students. At the first conversation in Rendsburg in Schleswig-Holstein, there were intense debates on Christianity and Existentialism. Names such as Heidegger, Jaspers and Sartre turned up all the time. Also, of course the name Sören Kierkegaard, whose writings were reminders of true Christianity and deeply impressed me.

Intellectual Experiences

In Lund, I had been confronted with the debate; "Belief and Knowledge", set forth in Ingemar Hedenius' book with the same title *Tro och vetande*, where he attempted to break apart all established Church doctrines. To have the opportunity to listen to him and his opponent Anders Nygren; each defending their non-Christian and

Christian standpoints, was a true intellectual experience. After listening to Hedenius, my friend Göran Laurell and I, being very well read in Swedenborg, and belonging to the New Church, concluded we had to give Hedenius his right. It was really wrong to set reason in subjection and obedience to belief.

It was through Swedenborg's message that everything fell into place about Christian doctrine. At the same time, the temptations to slide into atheism, agnosticism or resentment towards true Christianity truly diminished. I am also glad that much later in Stockholm, when I worked in the Societies of Religious studies of Humanism, I was involved in calling Hedenius to speak and converse on his book *Helvetet* (Hell), which I really believed to be a deserving cause,

In Lund, I listened often to the Professor in the Exegesis of the New Testament, Hugo Odeberg, who along with studying the symbolism of Jewish mysticism had also studied Swedenborg and this to a large extent formed his fascinating expositions of Biblical texts. In the spirit of Swedenborg, Odeberg often argued that "The Divine 'I am'", both in the New and in the Old Testament signifies the same, namely Christ, and his little book *Kristus och Skriften* can be seen as a very clear summation of the most important point in Swedenborg's doctrine on Holy Scripture. A certain competition ensued among the two of us in borrowing volumes of Swedenborg's *Arcana Coelestia* from the University Library. (In time of course I aquired these books for myself.)

The study of certain books by August Strindberg, to begin with, *Inferno*, and "*På Hafsstranden*" (*On the Sea shore*), by Vilhelm Ekelund, were important stimuli to study Swedenborg. From India, Sadhu Sundar Singh's little book *Syner från andevärlden...* (*Visions of the Spirtual World*), with direct reference to Swedenborg in Nathan Söderbloms preface, were also very significant to me. Soon I discovered the nineteenth century author Carl Jonas Love Almqvist as a permanent soul mate – he was for a time president of the Swedenborgian society in Stockholm, Pro fide et caritate.

Profound Encounter

The more profound encounter with Swedenborg's writings was something truly fantastic. In *True Christian Religion* I saw a clear thread through the whole Divine revelation collected in the message of "The One God", the glorified Jesus Christ: Father, Son and Holy Spirit in one Divine person. At the same time, I opened up to the great human value of this vision, on the Spiritual world and on the passage of human beings there meeting us. In Swedenborg's work *Heaven and Hell,* the cruel doctrine about the punishments of hell for those who were not saved, or who did not have the right faith disappeared.

The contradictions of the Bible which were seemingly cruel, or were scientifically untenable ideas also dissolved through Sweenborg's insistence on the Bible having an "inner sense", where the "spiritual sense" is the essential but at the same time he strongly held that the "literal sense" in the most important books of the Bible was fully inspired. The letter was then entirely representative and significative, while the "inner sense" of it is now through Divine revelation, was revealed to him to enunciate to humanity.

My need for rationality, humanity, consequential love and charity as highest principles, could now be combined with my need for the supersensous, for steadfastness in faith, for "fundamentalism". The attraction to Catholicism in academic circles now emerged rather visibly, but in spite of some advantages there, in comparison to Protestantism, nothing could convince me that the Catholic view had solved the inner conflicts of traditional Christianity as brilliantly as Swedenborg's "New Church" Christianity. The results of the Second Vatican Council would have made a rejection of Catholicism more difficult for me, but my choice would have remained clear. Also, I have always had an instinctive feeling that spiritual giant monoliths, such as the Catholic Church, as well as all State Churches, in themselves must be derailed spiritually because they exclude the true and invisible Kingdom of God, which among humans represents true religion.

All Religions are a path to God

Swedenborg, on the other hand, clearly taught me that the Lord in his Divine Providence turns spiritually dead institutions into his instruments, in a similar manner as all religions of the world in the same way are paths to God, paths for human beings to a life as angels in Heaven.

My appetite for studying various humanistic and theological subjects was great and my interest in studying Swedenborg only grew. In time, I managed to receive a good academic degree in Latin, Semitic languages (Hebrew and Arabic) and the History of Religions.

The emphasis in my studies in religious history was Graeco-Roman, Hellenistic, religion. Soon I was also preparing to become a preacher full time in the New Church, without knowing if this was going to be possible to realize in practise. The Summer of 1948 I had joined "Sällskapet Nya Kyrkans Bekännare" and had inspiring contact with its leading man, pastor Erik Hjerpe.

Involvment in New Church Societies

In 1949, I joined "The New Church Swedish Society" in Stockholm. In 1950, I began to now and then preach in Swedenborg's Memorial Church at Tegnérlunden in Stockholm. Jack Hårdstedt had become a priest of the society there and I assisted him at several occassions, for instance when he returned to Egypt to organize a Society of the New Church. In 1951, I was at a European New Church priestly meeting in Lausanne, Switzerland, togehether with the German speaking priestly candidate Friedemannn Horn, authorized to give services within "The General Convention of the New Jerusalem". The act was led by the leading Pastor Adolf L. Goerwitz who then was their European leader.

Ordination into the Lord's New Church

My contact with the New Church in Jönköping, however did not end and I was soon in close contact with the active New Church groups in Gothenburg. In 1952, I preached for the first time in this town. There I got deeper insight into the intense debates on doctrine going on in Jönköping during the 1930's, where the eighty year old New Church pastor Albert Björck in 1937 had spearheaded a society of the then newly formed international group "The Lord's New Church of the New Jerusalem".

After his passing his work was carried on by the excellent lay leader in town, Ryno Sigstedt. There one experienced a new view of the Lord's Word, where one unreservedly included Swedenborg's theological writings as "the Latin Word" or "the Third Testament", which was seen to have a literal sense on par with the Old and New Testaments. The deeper meaning was there to be seen only through a spiritual conversion of the human being and through enlightenment from the Lord alone. (Sacred Scripture #26)

When the letter of the Word is seen to be contradictory, reason can instead look for a representative or interior signifying sense. These thoughts also had eager proponents in the New Church in Gothenburg. I was early on captured by them, first through a little booklet by Charles Hotson, *Stand up for the Writings,* published in America. Later I was strongly stimulated in the same direction through contacts with the New Church pastors Ernest Pfeiffer and John Durban Odhner in Holland. I was also in contact with representatives of the same movement in the United States, foremost, the Rev. Theodor Pitcairn, whose sermons were sent to me and made a great impression on me.

I participated in the reorganization of pastor Björck's society in 1955-56, and came in contact with the members of the international "Nova Hierosolyma-Church" (The Lord's New Church which is Nova Hierosolyma). The organization was active foremost in the New Church in Holland.

A whole new period of theological studies now began on my part, both here at home and abroad, leading up to my ordination into the priesthood of the Lord's New Church. This took place at The Hague in Holland and was led by the then Church President Philip N. Odhner.

It pleases me to note that later on Philip Odhner became a Bishop, stemming in a direct descending line from the earlier mentioned, Pastor Jonas Odhner, who two hundred years ago enunciated the Lord's New Church message in Sweden.

*

The spiritual massage which Olle Hjern spent his whole life preaching and leading towards was to seek the Lord in His Word and bring His truths into life.

Rev Olle Hjern was an avid collector of books. Some he collected himself and some he inherited from early New Church Priests. There were many first editions and manuscripts of all sorts. It was in these early years, surrounded by his very large library in an apartment in Banérgatan on Östermalm, that he led the Society in Stockholm. He held services and large cultural gatherings, with invited speakers who spoke on a variety of religious themes which was spreading Swedenborg's cultural presence in the literary world in Sweden.,

There was usually an interesting speaker, after which people enjoyed bread, cheese and wine together, with good discussions. His five daughters were often there and his wife Inga shared these pleasant times also until her passing into the spiritual world in 1990. The last time a gathering was held there it was on the Dead Sea Scrolls and over a 100 people came, cramming the large rooms to the last seat.

Olle not only collected books but he also collected interesting people. A huge number of intellectuals, artists, poets and seekers visited Olle's home to hear of Swedenborg's doctrines and listen to the Word, among them, to mention a few, the artists Helga Henschen, Elisabeth Hermodsson, Mona Hellsing, Astrid Nyström, Tanja Perskaja, Josephine Siskind, Per Stahre and Magnus Malmsten.

Olle had collaborators who helped him with his journal *Världarnas möte – Nya Kyrkans tidning* (The Meeting of Worlds – New Church Journal), espescially Anders Hallengren, who was renowned for his many literary essays on Swedenborg and dissertation on Emerson.

Church services were later held in the Hartwick house, near Mariatorget and Swedenborg's own quarters in the Mullvaden block at Hornsgatan on Södermalm. For a time, in 1995 to 1999, a library was set up at Hornsgatan 60, next door to where Olle moved upon his retirement and where Eva Thunberg made a library catalog.

Olle continued to preach in Gothenburg and Arboga as well as leading the society in Stockholm. At some point, on his own initiative, he rented a place in Gröndal, just outside of Södermalm, and continued to have lectures, classes and services there between 2001 and 2009. It was here that he was assisted by a young literary woman, Susanna Åkerman, and whom he soon married.

Gröndal was supported by the Lord's New Church and Olle continued to preach there. In 2008, a new priestly colleague, Rev. Andrei Vashestov, came to work in Stockholm and he became pastor there after Olle passed into the spiritual world. Before that the activities had moved to Skanstull in Stockholm city with the new name Swedenborg Forum.

Olle's interest in culture stemmed from his upbringing in Jönköping, where his father Gunnar was principal of the local art and crafts school and his mother Edith made the home a center of beauty and applied arts.

It was his striving to constantly know more and embrace and delight in the creative energy in all the people he met that made him a very special person. The effort of his life was to spread the truths of the New Church.

Olle became an institution of the New Church to whom everyone turned to learn about Swedenborgianism in Sweden. He is dearly missed!

Skara Swedenborgianism
The Early Beginnings of the New Church

Olle Hjern

Westergötland is a Province in Southwestern Sweden that for many years hosted within its borders religious movements of an independent character, sometimes in opposition to the State religion. Perhaps this was true already in "heathen" times, as the Christian opposition took its primary hold in these lands in the late 10th century. Later on, however, in the States more severe Protestant times there were also problems with the Westrogothians.

These spiritual movements that were seeking an inner understanding of religious life, and awakening experiences of the "mystical union" of humans with God, went hand in hand with radical Pietist efforts to put the purity of life before the purity of doctrine. These movements were more and more a worry to the power seeking Lutheran Orthodoxy, because these strivings were sometimes mixed with outright "heretical" doctrines. In this context, we can recall from Luteran Orthodoxy, the strongly deviant German mystic Jacob Boehme.

Many of these radical tendencies were personified in one learned and pious man, who in the years 1702 to 1735, took the Bishop's seat in Skara, namely Bishop Jesper Svedberg. These radical tendencies of the Bishop were not without problems in regard to his position in the Swedish Lutheran Church, but his continued good connection with the Royal family contributed to his feeling of safety. He seems to have had an unshakable belief in Divine Providence and he totally rejected and was in opposition to the accepted norm of Lutheran belief in the doctrine of faith without the need of works.

Svedberg lived in close contact with beings in the other world, with angels and spirits. In the work, *America Illuminata,* he expresses concern for the innocense of the indians in America that could be spoiled through contact with profligate Christians. This is something entirely different than the usual Christian concern for the salvation of heathen souls. Such statements of course agree closely with those of his son Emanuel, who felt a Divine calling to mediate to humanity, which also resonated well with some of Jacob Boehme's writings.

As is known, Swedberg's son Emanuel had a Divine calling in 1743, to declare to the world a new and reformed Christianity, built on a revelation of the "Inner meaning of the Word". Within the Holy Scriptures he revealed a deeper and separate message than what is in the letter of the Word.

In 1749, Emanuel Swedenborg began to publish his writings in large Latin volumes in London. In the next twenty years, the amount of readers and followers of his writings were very sparse. However, in the latter part of the 1760's there began to be a certain degree of change.

Both in London, England and in Gothenburg, Sweden, new friends and acquaintances began to try to spread Swedenborg's message. In both places this provoked opposition. In Gothenburg, a small but strong group formed, who were mostly part of the people who worked with the Swedish East-Indian Company. Most known among them were Beyer and Rosén, who were seen as dangerous to the State because of their official positions of educating future priests. Also, in this circle belonged the merchant, Lars Lindström, who was to become a prominent person in Skara. In 1767, Lindström had already been pointed as leader of a new spiritual movement.

A little later, In Swedenborg's correspondence with friends in Gothenburg, he mentions various dramatic events; where there is talk of a psychically gifted boy in Skara, who was in conscious contact with the spiritual world and who had learned medical methods to treat people. Swedenborg answered that he was willing to take care of the boy and to answer for his schooling, but said that the boy was too young to deliver meaningful medial contacts with the other world.

The event at least shows early contacts between Swedenborg's friends in Gothenburg and people in Skara. As a witness to this is also a

54

handwritten translation of Swedenborg's *Conjugial Love*, done by the mentioned Beyer and with an interesting note at the end: "This book was given to me by my beloved father. (Skara, 12th of July 1782), Anna Beata Lindström". This manuscript is in our archives in Stockholm, now deposited in the Royal Library. And it could well have been done during Swedenborg's lifetime. The said note was written at the time of the passing away of the father, Lars Lindström. Lindström's daughters were long well known in the Swedenborgian circle.

Another launching point for Swedenborgianism in the Skara dioscese were lively debates among priests and laity, concerning the Christian doctrine on atonement and justification.

In the 1760's, the lecturer, P. C. Wahlfelt, was reported to the state for theological errors, in spite of the fact that his thinking was in the same direction as that of his supervisor the Dioscesan pastor, Anders Olofsson Knös. They both had argued forcefully against the traditional Church doctrines of God's wrath, and the Son's vicarious atonement to remove the wrath of the Father. They also argued about the relationship between faith and works. Wahlfelt and Knös more and more came to identify their standpoints with Swedenborg's message. Their positive interest in Swedenborg appears to have become a great wave of influence among the priests of the Diocese. In this, Knös' being established as a spirtual leader was of great value. The teachers at Skara Gymnasium School were strongly influenced by him and very much appreciated his conversation. In the gatherings on Sunday nights, more and more people were brought into his direction of thought. The thought of the suffering of God's son, in the vicarious atonement, came to be seen as a gruesome doctrine that obscures God's love and makes the persons in the Godhead separate gods.

There were eager studies of Swedenborg's Latin works, but also many handwritten translations circulated in the district. A very central person for this movement was Leonard Gyllenhaal, lord at the manor Höberg. He was a military man and a scientist. He is known to have produced such handwritten manuscripts. The same is true of the priest, Jonas Pehrsson Odhner, who was first in Varnhem and then in

Mariestad. He produced a Swedish translation of Swedenborg's *True Christian Religion*. It was published in Copenhagen in 1795, because of the Laws of Publication in Sweden, Swedenborg's works could not be published in Sweden.

In spite of a weak public presence – and of the many priests and functionaries of the Church who were reluctant to even mention the name Swedenborg – the Swedenborg inspired spiritual movement appears to have been very strong and did actually have an enormous effect in the cultural life in our country.

We get a lively picture of the movement's influence from the memoirs of Arvid August Afzelius, 'Minnen', which was postumously first published in 1901. In this memoir he describes his studies as a youth, when he was in close contact with priests who were then generally admired: Jonas and his father, Pehr Hemming Odhner, and also the family Knös, in Skara.

Carl Johan Knös, son of Anders Knös, was a dedicated New Church believer. He worked as a principal at the Skara Gymnasium. With recommendations from him, Afzelius as a young man, was able to go to study in Uppsala. At the university he immediately came into contact with a relative, another Westrogothian, who was a well known Swedenborgian and also a pioneer in Africa, Adam Afzelius, a Professor at the University.

In Uppsala, Afzelius led what can be called a Linnean-Swedenborgian Society, where also the theologian Pehr Hemming Odhner was a central member. Also, they were joined by the Westrogothian Jurist, Lars Herman Gyllenhaal, from Härlingstorp, a man who also had close contacts with the New Church circle in Stockholm and had also close connnection to Westergötland. Afzelius reported about New Church services held in Stockholm at Carl Johan Schönherr's house, at Packartorget square (now Norrmalmstorg). Schönherr was a leading person in the 'Westrogothian leaning', New Church society, Pro Fide et Caritate, (For Faith and Charity).

Also arriving from Skara to Uppsala was Gustaf Knös, who is called a "Swedenborgian central person". He was son of Anders Olofsson Knös and a Professor at the University in Eastern languages. He was something of a mystic, which is reflected in the title of his meditative work, in the Swedenborgian spirit: *Conversations with myself on the soul, man and God* (Part I, 1824, Part II, 1827). The second part of his work contained a defence of Swedenborg's doctrines, where he also defined the "Westrogothian Swedenborgianism" and its view of the Church Society as non-separatist. His wife Alida came from the New Church family, Olbers, in Gothenburg. Alida, through her literary interests, was to become an important person in the social circles of the Romantics, in Uppsala.

In 1795, Levin Olbers, a "Swedenborgian" from Gothenburg, was appointed Professor of Theology in Uppsala. In 1814, Levin moved to Skara, to take up the position as Dioscesan Pastor, he actually got a fellow believer from Westrogothia, Sven Lundblad, as successor to his professorship. It is said that he was fascinated by the Swedenborgian thoughts regularly found in the conversations at the gatherings of Anders Knös, in Skara. Eventually, Lundblad became Bishop of Skara and his cathecetic major work *Christna Religionens Hufvudläror* (*Main Doctrines of the Christian Religion*) in 1825, reached a broad readership. It was strongly coloured by Swedenborg's thoughts, perhaps also by Plato's. It was also translated into German. Lundblad became legendary. He was from very humble origins and died as Bishop in 1837.

There are many descriptions of the warm friendship, and the intense interest in culture and education that was present in people counted as 'Skara' Swedenborgians. Of course, those who were cultured and literary, with philosophical and scientific interests, worked to raise the spiritual and educational level of the common people in the vicinity. Such aspects of these circumstance can be known through the wonderful work of Anna Frederika Ehrenborg and her book, *Anteckningar till det husliga livet*, (*Notes for Domestic Life*) written in 1845. Gathered around Bishop Lundblad were fellow believers who believed in the importance of the Dioscese. Such names as: – Carl Johan Knös, Anna Frederika Ehrenborg, Leonard Gyllenhaal and

Pehr Hemming Odhner. Others also moved down to Skara from Stockholm, including Carl Johan Schönherr with families. Here and there by the manors, schools were built, the blessings of which I myself received, and now continue with my own family tradition.

Also, at the same period of time in Lund a Westrogothian Swedenborgian was appointed Professor, namely Anders Jakob Hellstenius. He was from Skara and during his gymnasium experience had received deep impressions of a Swedenborgian direction. His most important contribution as a Swedenborgian was perhaps to awaken his brother in Law, Achatius Kahl, (a university teacher in Eastern languages), to take an interest in his views and beliefs. Becuse Kahl later wrote, *Nya Kyrkan och dess betydelse för theologins studium i Sverige*, (*The New Church and its impact on the Study of Theology in Sweden*), a work containing interesting aspects of the Westrogothians.

We have to ask the question, what is the real origin of Skara Swedenborgianism. A case against a heretic priest, Sven Schmidt, clearly shows that the Skara movement was alive and well during Swedenborg's life time.

From investigating written family traditions, we have come to the impression that the strongest motivations must have stemmed from Emanuel Swedenborg's pastor at the Swedish Church in London, Arvid Ferelius. Ferelius is said to have asked sharp questions to Swedenborg before administring a private Holy supper in the last year of his life; questions such as whether what Swedenborg had said about the other world was true or fiction? In reply, Swedenborg gave him a most convincing answer about the full truth of all that he had written.

After his period of service in London, Ferelius became priest in Skövde and soon was convinced of the truth of Swedenborg's spiritual message. His daughters established homes that became true seed beds for New Church Christianity. In the genealogical book *Två släkter* (Two families) by Hedda Ekman, we can read of Arvid Ferelius that "it was through him that the greater families, as well as the Westrogothians in general, joined Swedenborgianism". As spokesman, Hedda Ekman here refers to another of his descendants, no less than the very prominent historian Harald Hjärne in Uppsala.

His daughter Helena had written a Swedenborgian Cathechism for children and the book presented a religious and fine tuned perspective of her being in the same spiritual spirit. She married a New Church central figure in Stockholm, the silk manufacturer, Carl Johan Schönherr, who also began offering religious services in the capitol city. In time, he moved to Sparresäter in Westergötland and similarily became an important spiritual figure in this lands end. His first wife, who was Ferelius' daughter, had already passed into the other world. He loved the beautiful natural landscape when he arrived there. He saw in it a mirroring of the other world and became more and more inspired. Leonard Gyllenhaal, his good friend and fellow spirit, was also inspired to do his scientific work on plants and insects there.

In the summer of 1786, a group of famous Swedenborgians gathered in Sweden - among them were August Nordenskiöld, Carl Bernhard Wadström, Christian Johansén, Brita Knös and her son Olof Knös - at *Himmelskällan*, the Heaven's Well in Varnhem, to drink water. As a result of this, an Exegetic and Philantropic Society was formed, with requirements for the members to declare belief in the Divinity of Swedenborg's writings and to contribute to their spread by all means. August Nordenskiöld, also early on, wanted to prepare the way for an independent separated Swedenborgian Church Society. The Westrogothians were from the very beginning actually, a very important part of this Society. Their regular meeting place was, however, to be located in Stockholm.

The following year a message arrived from London of a newly established society in the name of the New Church, completely separate from other denominations. The leader of this New Church Society, Robert Hindmarsh, had received a critical rejoinder from the powerful preacher John Clowes in Manchester. [1]

Clowes was an avid translator of Swedenborg and was one hundred percent preaching a representative of Swedenborg's revealed message, but he was completely against the separatist stance. His many writings were partly translated and were certainly studied in Westrogothia.

A Liturgy for the New Church, mainly a translation from the new Society in London, was eventually published in Stockholm, but it received harsh criticism by Gustaf Knös in the second part of *Samtal med mig sjelf... (Conversations with myself...)* The whole family Knös was apparently against the separatist tendency, even if they could be said to make virtue out of necessity.

A firm belief in the Divine Word, and the reality of the spiritual world and its presence and a belief in the Lord Jesus Christ as our only God and Saviour, was apparently self-evident for the Skara Swedenborgians. However, potentially controversial suggestions were also presented. In this connection, a conscious contact with the spiritual world was made, with spirits from the other side. They are mentioned in Anna Frederika Ehrenborg's early publications, especially in the Journal *Något Nytt (Something New)*. Communication with automatic writing from contacted spirits was not unusual. A great deal of this information is still preserved, derived from the priestly family Synnerholm, in Undenäs, and Ferelius' relatives and Swedenborgian believers.

In close contact with the people in Westergötland, was the Swedenborgian inspired author, Carl Jonas Love Almqvist. He was a member of Pro Fide et Caritate and a friend of Pehr Hemming Odhner in Uppsala, together, according to what he said, they read through all of the writings of Swedenborg.

In the book *Det går an (It is permitted)*, the main character Sara Videbäck says when she and Albert passes by 'Råbäck':

> *"Råbäck! I have heard Råbäck spoken of! I have not been there before, [...],*
> - *But why should I now go there, when she no longer lives there?*
> - *Which she?*
> - *That was where an angel lived, who has now moved to Vättern lake.*

    - *Mrs... I know... I do not remember the name.*

    - *I have not seen her either, Sara continued, but if she still lived in Råbäck then I would like to take that road. Good, excellent books, she lent to Aunt Gustava in Lidköping, and we have read them together in spare moments."*

It is evident here that Anna Frederika Ehrenborg is meant, who recently moved from Råbäck to Kråk, on the Westrogothian side of lake Vättern. This is the key to the whole story, which then lets Sara's female wisdom ultimately stem from Swedenborg's writings, foremost of course from *Conjugial Love.*

No one in our country has popularized Swedenborg's doctrines as much as Mrs. Ehrenborg, who wrote a series of books and journals, with well preseved dimension and depth. Almqvist was a personal friend of hers, but when *Det går an,* was published she had not yet stepped forward as a fullfledged writer. With her Journal *Något Nytt,* and later *Ett Christligt Sändebud (A Christian Herald),* she was to prepare the way for the first public appearance of the New Church in Sweden. Perhaps she was to change her earlier "non-separatist" view in the spirit of Gustaf Knös. Mrs. Ehrenborg corresponded with a close friend and fellow believer in Denmark, Julie Corriring, who had completed Immanuel Tafel's translation into German of Swedenborg's *Arcana Coelestia.* Both of these women can, with good reason, be seen as having given the most important stimulus to the organization of the New Church in Denmark and Sweden.

In this case, the German-American Latin Professor R L Tafel's Scandinavian visit must have meant a great deal. He came to Sweden to look for and publish all documents concerning Swedenborg and he received a friendly reception by Anna Frederika Ehrenborg and her son in law, the Bishop Ebbe Bring in Linköping. Tafel represented the strong Swedenborgian separatism and High Church stance that would later be organized in the New Church Academy in Philadelphia, Pennsylvania, and in the General Church of the New Jerusalem. He also had Anna Frederika Ehrenborg take back her earlier occultist writings. She died in 1873, when the small organized societies of the New Church, with her support, had begun to form in Denmark as well as in Sweden.

These times were no doubt benevolent to free church activity, and a strong branch of free thinking was led by E J Ekman and P P Waldenström, known for their preaching on the "subjective" doctrine of atonement which showed great similarities to the message of Emanuel Swedenborg, spread by Anders Knös.

In the middle of the 1870's a group was formed in Stockholm called Sällskapet för Nya Kyrkans Bekännare (*The Society of New Church Confessors*), that long served as an organiziational unit for the New Church. It had many members in Westrogothia, among them the priest Sanfrid Odhner in Herrljunga, and the family Flach, on Prinshaga in Axvall.

This society hired a priest, the Norwegian born Adolph Theodor Boyesen, educated in America, and it was reported that he was preaching the New Church message in cooperation with Odhner in Herrljunga. Sanfrid was son of Pehr Hemming Odhner and he was to send his nephew Carl Theophilus Odhner over to America to study under a New Church pastor at the New Church Academy in Philadelphia. He later became a most prominent priest and theologian there. [2] In Pennsylvania, the descendants of the Westrogothian Swedenborgians are great in number, both those with the name Odhner, and those with the name Gyllenhaal. Their ancestral belief is still alive and well with them.

The Swedenborgian movement lost momentum in the latter part of the 1800's, but still the Skara dioscese had a great deal of Christian believers with this Swedenborgian interest. Up to 1865, there was in Fröjered the philanthropist and Swedenborgian pastor Johan Sundblad. In the same society, Gunnar Wetterberg, served as pastor until 1955. He was in close contact with the New Church organizations in Stockholm and he was one of my close friends. He was a devoted first hand, "orthodox" follower of Swedenborg's spiritual message. He was to step forth with Swedenborg's message in many circles, until his death in 1972.

Among the the Westrogothian cultural personalities in the 1800's, connected to this movement, was the jurist J. G. Rickert, who was the father of our parliamentarian constitution. He was married to Ferelius' grand daughter. And then Johannes Sundblad who was an author and ethnologist and in his later years was active in the organized New Church. The Hope is that the future of the New Church will continue to see the fruitful results of these early movements and see the continued growth of Swedish culture and spirituality.

---

[1] John Clowes (1743-1831) from the 1770's to his death, in Manchester and Lancashire led a strong Swedenborgian movement, whose social consciousness was expressed in the building of schools and for the first time putting to practise the cooperative idea. A contemporary similar activity in Sweden can be connected to the priests Jonas Pehrsson Odhner (1744-1830) and his son Pehr Hemming Odhner (1790-1857), both as with Clowes, translators of Swedenborg. Especially the latter, priest at Horn in the Skara Diocese, and an excellent preacher, can also be called a central person in the Swedenborgian spiritual movement.
[2] A son of Carl Theophilus Odhner, Philip N Odhner, became Swedenborgian Bishop in America and a considerable theologian and Church leader. He passed away as late as 20 December 1998, almost ninety years old.

Ivan Aguéli
His unique style of art made him one of the founders of the Swedish modern art movement.

The Landscape as a State of the Soul –
On Swedenborg's importance for Ivan Aguéli

Olle Hjern

Ivan Aguéli was tireless in his studies of various ideologies, mythologies and religious doctrines. Apparently, he first came to know Swedenborg through circles of the New Church in Stockholm, where he frequently socialized at Reverend Adolph Theodor Boyesen's home, located at Observatoriegatan 22. Axel Gauffin's biography of Ivan Agueli mentions that Ivan got a useful and grateful opponent in Einar, the pastor's son, in the tough sport and art of fencing with sabres. This sport was successfully acted out in a backyard in the district of Vasastan. Agueli continued to keep contact with members of the Boyesen family for a long time. During this time, Einar's son, Björn became an active priest in the New Church.

Ivan's studies in Swedenborg's works must have been especially thorough, as almost all of Swedenborg's writings are commented on in his letters. While Ivan was studying in France, he was drawn to all forms of mysticism including Sufism, the mysticism of Islam. However, he never abandoned Swedenborg and held fast to the essential truths he had learned from Swedenborg until his death. Thus, Ivan remained "a Swedenborgian" after passing over to Islam. Apparently, his primary effort was to discover eternal truths within the revelations of all major religions. He had learned some of these truths through initiation into "esoteric" circles, which he influenced to an important degree. Sometimes he called himself a "Swedenborgian anarchist". However, his anarchism was more akin to Tolstoy's mild doctrine which he highly admired, than with any tending to violence.

In Paris, Aguéli was introduced to a theosophical lodge which had a special concern for the study of the "hermetic science", "la science hermetique". This included thoughts on the correspondence of 'worlds': "That which is above is mirrored in an image of what is below". One of the members of this lodge explained later that "Aguéli's important contribution was his knowledge of Swedenborg, in whose writings he had long been immersed".

In prison for political reasons, Aguéli immersed himself deeply into Swedenborg's works. In a letter from prison, he emphasized the importance of the worship of only One God as previously defined by Swedenborg. Agueli explained "Monotheism is the highest hill of life, as it is belief in the highest force of life". In this same letter we can read the following:

"The canonical Christ is the incarnated Word – the Highest Being became man, according to St. John 1: 1-5 and 9-14... The relationship between the Father and Son in the Gospels corresponds to that between soul and body, Jesus Christ is the highest harmony between spirit and matter and the most beautiful symbolism for anti-hypocrisy, monotheism and compassion. The Compassion of the Soul means: Tolerance and forgiving, compassion and sacrifice. Try to understand that one can rise up by humbling oneself, and be victorious through suffering. By this means you will come to understand Christ."

Similarly, Aguéli saw the outer landscape and the outer environment in correspondence to the human soul, its incarnation and "morphing" in the soul of man. Baudelaire's poem "Correspondences", in *Les Fleurs du Mal,* carried special importance to Aguéli in this connection. The background of Baudelaire's poem dwells on Swedenborg's theory of correspondences. Aguéli wrote in a letter to a friend:

"All these studies in Art, Religion and Mythology, Philosophy, and Language, all this is with the great goal of Symbolism – the doctrine of Correspondences that reveals what is between the visible and the invisible, between spirit and matter, between the worlds of causes and effects – because it is in Symbols that the new world will live!"

In this letter, one notices that Swedenborg is behind every word. "Admit that a Landscape can represent a state of the soul", Aguéli says in a letter and continues: "The monotheistic landscape is very sunny, lit by a penetrating sun, by a light strong enough to let the perspective of air push out the perspective of lines, in that spirit dominates matter."

Art to Aguéli must mirror the true spiritual reality, expressed as living yet unmoving, with a character of eternity and stillness where each thing in a deeper dimension is given its right place, its real color or is put in its right place. Erik Blomberg underlines in his *Svenska målarpionjärer* how strongly Aguéli's whole view of landscapes and art is marked by religious mysticism.

In Blomberg's book there is an important article by Aguéli on his theory of art from the journal La Gnose in 1911. The article shows that the artist was strongly influenced by Islam, but still remained a vivid proponent of Swedenborg's doctrine of correspondences.

Among the papers the police found in Aguéli's living quarters after his arrest, there was a manuscript entitled *Suggestions de Swedenborg (Du ciel et de L'enfer).* – Suggestions by Swedenborg (on Heaven and Hell). This manuscript was divided into paragraphs which conformed to Swedenborg's "Heaven and Hell". The first paragraph in Argueli's manuscript stated:

"Revelation of the inner sense so that the wisdom that is of this world may not frighten the temple of heart and faith. – Ought one, in order to lead an artistically gifted child's education, reveal to him the science of correspondences?"

Ivan Aguéli's use of the correspondence theory was commented on by the Swedish poet Gunnar Ekelöf in an essay:

"What he seeks is something beyond the physical appearance, it is the world of form and numbers, it is the correspondence doctrine of colors, it is painting's awesome alchemy."

Closely connected to Aguèli in Paris was the young Swedish artist Olof Sager-Nelson, who was also deeply influenced by Swedenborg's thoughts. In the seemingly realistic pictorial representations of them both, they wanted to reveal a deeper reality, the world of dreams, and the spiritual world. In an exhibition catalogue, Evert Taube said, "A type of symbolism, something of "likenesses" reaches us through Sager-Nelson, and this is true both in his stricter formations and in his shimmering choice of color". This can without a doubt also be said of Ivan Aguéli.

Just as Sager-Nelson, Aguéli strongly experienced "the great seer's commandment on the impact of purifying pain" (Gauffin: Sager-Nelson) and the ideal for them both became Christ, as seen in the light of the Evangelists and in the representations of Swedenborg. Aguéli saw the life of Christ, as his own, as stated:

".... An unending fight against inherited instincts and the prejudices that he has from his earthly existence, his mother and his land; his enemies, the atavisms and their caretakers, and the traditions whose belief is a worship of monuments as fetishes.

The goal is rebirth, the return to the eternal Father through the higher movement or the primal beam which brings reception to the beauty of eternity."

This quotation is taken from Blomberg's *Svenska målarpionjärer*. In every word is mirrored Swedenborg's portrayal of the worldly temptations of the Lord, of His overcoming of the hells, of the evil spiritual forces, as well as His own weaker and purely natural human nature, the nature of Mary, during His fight and His victories and His glorification or deification in this world.

Aguéli did not believe in reincarnation in the usual sense. He believed that the purely material clothing of our spirit was something for a single use in this world, and from which we continuously go into a deeper dimension of existence. It is, he says in a letter, "as when you leave your outer coating during a journey from a cold country to a warm. "The spiritual world becomes conscious to us first in a wholehearted struggle for a true reality, when the Divine beam of rebirth strikes us."

He further says, in the above mentioned letter:

"It is the conjunction of the good and true, the active and the passive, a cross that is the formula of life and this beam I have talked to you about – an indispensable condition for rebirth. The beam should decide our eternal life. It is the seed to a life without end, and always growing and moving as it is spiritual and more or less directly affecting matter, as it is an inner life. – Why take back a discarded clothing? – Hell. That, which is heaven for one, is hell for another. Nothing is more relative than pleasure and pain."

Quite naturally one has regarded Aguéli's "Swedenborgian" period as an abandoned stage, as he more and more moved away from Christianity to fully embrace Islam. However, during his later years, he saw common values in what he had found in Swedenborg and through Islamic mysticism. In late letters he puts it in this way:

"Swedenborg has given me the mystical education through which I have defended myself against and which liberated me from all Protestantism and germanification – Mohyddin Ibn Arabi have given me the universal clarity, through certitude, mildness and strength.

Swedenborg was a great man and to find his match in spiritual enlightenment, we have to go back many centuries to the Orient. If we see past the name of Christ and away from names to things of reality, then we find Swedenborg's doctrines, for example, a great part of them and the most essential are confirmed since millennia.

I have worked on a study of the secret teachings of the Orient and when it is finished one shall see how great the similarities are between Swedenborg and the holy crowd of great souls: I speak about the saints and the men of God who even today protect the common man when he leaves this world and gets closer to God. When you see how these past spiritual generations come from secret doctrines in the temples of Egypt, Assyria and India and shine forth most clearly with the so called fakiers and derwishes and are being finalized by the Swedenborgian light, then one is close to seeing eternity before oneself.

It is much in Swedenborg that I do not accept; and some that I even reject and disapprove, but it is perhaps because I have not understood him, yet in any case, **Swedenborg is the clearest spirit that Europe has brought forth since the beginning of time."**

(The quotations are taken from Gauffin's and Blomberg's above mentioned studies.)

Vilhelm Ekelund
Swedish Author/Poet 1889 - 1949

Religiosity and Spirituality with Vilhelm Ekelund

Olle Hjern

It is not easy to define what religiosity is, but one can define the concept as an inner bond to a higher power or to an experience of a life in a higher dimension. The Swedish author, Vilhelm Ekelund, truly belongs to the list of deeply living religious human beings; also in a high degree to those who can show each of us the path to a deeper life. Ekelund is the author of *"På Hafsstranden* – On the Sea shore" – studying Swedenborg's perceptions of the world.

Vilhelm Ekelund for over half a century gained nourishment in the study of Emanuel Swedenborg. His works have become a powerful help to the daily search and practice of Swedenborg's spiritual message in life. According to Swedenborg, the path to realize a true Christian love in this world is to constantly and regularly examine oneself and then immediately seek to flee evil, or the evil act, whenever it comes one's way.

In the same spirit, Ekelund shows us happiness is in a wholehearted striving, and how it is a liberating to lay off the power of selfishness and how we can come into a peaceful state of creative life through this honest striving and openhearted strife.

At the same time saying that we must always be on guard against the selfishness and the downward powers that are constantly around us pulling us down. According to Swedenborg, we are regenerated by taking responsibility for ourselves and by steadily and conscientiously going through temptations and spiritual battles that our earthly existence brings.

The same thought is found in Ekelund, who also stresses the clear-sightedness that the overcoming of self brings. According to Ekelund, to die for oneself in a 'New Testament' way, is to walk the way of the cross and he sees this as the only door for us to enter real creative life, where a higher life can flow in.

Ekelund often refers to the writings of the great mystics. He often uses their language and presents them as guides along the path. He urges us to always first seek "the Kingdom of God" and to daily cleanse out all which pulls us down in our lives". He reminds us steadily that only through true humility can there be a foundation for creative greatness. "Through death is life", is an old saying that is known in different religions and even by those with different views. Also, in accordance with Swedenborg, Ekelund warns us against letting the Christian tradition have monopoly on true religiosity.

However, Ekelund, in his toned down attitude has been able to de-scribe the heights of mystical experience. He is not alone in this, yet there is something unique in him. As no one else, he shows us the way to a mystical life in the midst of the negative forces of this world. He stresses that we do not have to enter a monastery, we do not have to flee this world in an outer way – if things go bad the evils of this world can enter us through our imagined sense of self. - But at the same time Ekelund is far from generalizing. Our inner path to spiritual light, to the sunshine of the spirit can certainly be opened through various outer behaviors. It is the inner honesty and the who-lehearted sincerity that decides. One also senses in Ekelund a strong sense that a higher inspiration is present, not only in old religious writings, but also where spiritual people with less worldly demands have set their footprints.

Havsvåg
av Ann Frössén

Personally, I must say that the writings of Vilhelm Ekelund have always had a strong affect on me and spiritually driven me down on my knees before an inscrutable higher power - before the Lord God. This experience has always been strong but without any tendency to make me want to flee from this world. Instead the experience has given me the power to freely and securely go face the things of life once more, even with its often complicated human relations. There is truly here a message in accordance with the New Testament, of 'being in the World, but not of this world'. I myself want to call this experience mysticism in its most honest form. It is not hostile to the enjoyments of life or to intellectual diversity, but urges us to always concentrate on the higher values of life and what is spiritually meaning to us. If we sincerely seek and listen to our inner voice, we shall find what Ekelund is stating. Thus, that in life, our victory in spiritual battles also becomes one with an inner quiet - in the deepest sense.

Ekelund's message helps us to overcome the smaller or greater irritations in our life and be objective to the feelings of rage against misstreatments of ourselves. Also to overcome the often anxious defense of ourselves and instead seek guidance from higher truth and light. In this context, this message of classical wisdom teaches us of the right measure of temperance, of inner balance and about self-control!

With Vilhelm Ekelund there is always a profound respect for the sacred in our existence. He recognizes the true beauty in creation and in human life. He can lift us up in times when so much seems sunken down into darkness. His is a rejuvenating force and would be valuable to the churches and religions of this world.

He does not deny the importance of rational thinking and sees the importance of analyzing ourselves concerning our own situation. At the same time, he wants to show us the way to a more profound spiritual sense of sight, toward a vision of heavenly light which lies in the background shadow of this phenomenal world.

Ekelund wanted to be a guide to a deeper spiritual dimension and to me this has meant a new vision of the message of Emanuel Swedenborg. Also to acknowledge others who are representing high spiritual values.

In the same spirit, Vilhelm Ekelund speaks in his own terms of how we can be led into in a spiritual experience with secure safety under a Divine Providence.

Out of Body Experiences in the Light of Emanuel Swedenborg

Olle Hjern

Swedenborg – Scientist and "Spirit seer"

When the author, Raymond Moody in the 1970's set focus on people's near death and out-of-body experiences, it is rather natural that he refers to a Swedish man who in the past had a lot to say on the subject, namely Emanuel Swedenborg. Swedenborg was a scientist and spirit-seer. He was born in 1688 in Stockholm, Sweden where he lived the greater part of his life, however he traveled often to the Netherlands and to London. He died in London in 1772.

Swedenborg's Background

As a young man, Swedenborg dedicated himself to the study of natural science and was active for many years in the Swedish College of Mines. He was also known for his many technical inventions and scientific research. Actually in his research on the human brain, he made a monumental discovery that the higher functions of the brain are located in the cortex. His analysis did not concur with Descartes much earlier description of the brain. However, Swedenborg's prediction was correct, but it was not confirmed and validated until two hundred years later.

Swedenborg relentlessly researched and wrote about the nature of the human soul and its survival after death. In 1740 he went through several spiritual experiences which resulted in him having a religious transformation. It was during this crisis that he experienced a Divine calling to reveal to mankind the nature of the spiritual world and to make public to the world a message of a reformed New Christianity.

This Divine calling directed Swedenborg to make public "the inner meaning of the Word", and the hidden, "esoteric", truth behind its literal sense. A spiritual meaning to the Bible was not an unknown concept in the then present Christian Church. Many before him had attempted to translate an inner meaning of the Bible. Swedenborg's Doctrine of Correspondences however, surpasses any study ever written on the inner meaning of the Word.

During Swedenborg's youth, a belief in supernatural manifestations of the spiritual world in daily life flourished in Sweden. Swedenborg's father, Jesper Swedberg, lived in a world of constant signs, visions, and other supernatural appearances. When Swedenborg, who was a well-known honored statesman and scientist, suddenly published the results of his spiritual calling; and expounded publicly on his connection to the world of spirits, there must have been surprise, if not astonishment.

Swedenborg's books detail how he had been admitted to the spiritual world, his conversations with spirits and angels, explaining how everything is arranged in a Divine order and giving a living reality to the spirit world, never seen before.

Even during Swedenborg's time, there were discussions of out-of-body phenomena from a religious and historical perspective. These influences most likely came, in part, from the stories told of miracles in the New Testament and in the old legends of saints. There was also influence from the religious practices of the older population in Northern Scandinavia. Swedenborg's own teacher, Olof Rudbeck, the elder, was knowledgeable about the old practices and beliefs and participated in these religious discussions, as did Swedenborg himself. Additionally, there was much interest of an earlier work, *Lapponia* (1673), by Johannes Scheffer. This was a surprisingly modern work for the time, which documented Shamanism of the northern peoples and their journeys outside the body.

Scheffer's work specifically discussed experiences of individuals among the northern peoples, who were said to "spontaneously" fall into a sort of ecstasy during which they became unconscious of their outer senses and movements. In this state, onlookers had a concern with the safety of the body. However, when they came back to their senses again, they were unharmed and it is told were able to point out robberies and tell secrets one wanted, or did not want exposed. Swedenborg was interested in such cases from a psychological point of view. His intent was to find out what special gifts and techniques were utilized to arrive at such an ecstasy. He observed that it seemed to be connected to slowing down circulation of the blood and controlled breathing.

Swedenborg's Breathing Technique

Swedenborg had previously utilized a technique of intense concentration and meditation enabling him come into a state of "inner breathing". He did this by a certain holding back of outer respiration and thereby experienced standing on the threshold to a higher world. In time, Swedenborg utilized "inner breathing" or the "respiration of the soul" as a path to out-of-body experiences. This was accomplished by coming into a unison breathing with beings on a higher and more interior plane, where by he became part of the spirit community in a conscious way, while remaining here in earthly life.

Swedenborg stated, "Sometimes, too, I have been restricted to nothing but the breathing of my spirit, and then was sensibly aware of its harmony with the general breathing of heaven. On any number of occasions, too, I have been in a state like that of angels and have been lifted up to them in heaven; and at times like these I was in the spirit and out of the body, using my breathing to talk with them just as we do in this world. These and other firsthand proofs have made it clear to me not only that our spirits are breathing within our bodies, but also that they do so after we leave our bodies behind; and that the breathing of our spirits is so subtle that we do not sense it. It flows into the obvious breathing of our bodies almost the same way a cause flows into an effect or a thought flows into the lungs and through the lungs into speech." (DLW 391) Dole[1]

Naturally, one thinks in this context of the yogis of India and their breathing techniques that also are aimed at attaining conjunc-

---

1 E Swedenborg, *Angelic Wisdom on Divine Love and Wisdom* nr 391,
  Sw Transl. by Sevén-Lind, Stockholm 1926, s 272.

tion with a higher world. At the same time, there is no evidence that Swedenborg had any knowledge of the yogis of India.

Swedenborg's View on his Experiences - In 1749, he divided his experiences into two types:

"There are two kinds of visions that are not of the ordinary kind, into which I have been let solely that I might know their nature, and what is meant by it being said in the Word that men were "withdrawn from the body," and that they were "carried by the spirit into another place."" (AC 1882)

"As regards to the first experience, namely being withdrawn from the body, the case is this":

"The man is brought into a certain state that is midway between sleep and wakefulness, and when he is in this state he cannot know but that he is wholly awake. All his senses are as fully awake as in the highest wakefulness of the body; the sight, the hearing, and, wonderful to say, the touch, which is then more exquisite than it can ever be in the wakefulness of the body. In this state also spirits and angels have been seen to the very life, and also heard, and, wonderful to say, have been touched, and almost nothing of the body then intervened. This is the state of which it is said that they are "withdrawn from the body," and that they "do not know whether they are in the body or out of it." I have been let into this state only three or four times, merely that I might know how the case is with it, and that spirits and angels are in the enjoyment of every sense, even touch in a form more delicate and more exquisite than that of the body." (AC 1883)

Swedenborg drew parallels between this type of experience and the statement of Paul in the Second Corinthians, chapter twelve where we read:

"I knew a man in Christ above fourteen years ago, (whether in the body, I cannot tell; or whether out of the body, I cannot tell: God knowth). Such a one was caught up to the third heaven. He was

---

2 E Swedenborg, *Arcana Coelestia* (Heavenly Secrets) nr. 1882, vol. 3
    transl Sevén, Kristianstad 1866, p 314.

78

caught up into paradise, and heard unspeakable words, which it is not lawful for a man to utter." 2 Corinth 12: 2-4 (KJV)

The second type of experience Swedenborg described in the following manner:

"As regards the other kind of vision-being carried away by the spirit into another place - it has been shown me by living experience what it is, and how it is done, but only two or three times. One single experience I may mention. Walking through the streets of a city and through the country, and being at the same time also in conversation with spirits, I did not know but that I was wide awake and saw as at other times, so that I walked on without mistake, and all the time being in vision, seeing groves, rivers palaces, houses, men, and many other things. But after I had thus walked for hours, suddenly I was in the sight of the body, and became aware that I was in another place. Greatly amazed at this, I perceived that I had been in such a state as they were in of whom it is said that they were "led away by the spirit into another place;" for while this state lasts there is no reflection concerning the way, even if it be many miles; nor is there reflection concerning the time, even if it be many hours or days; nor is there any feeling of fatigue. Moreover the person is led through ways of which he has no knowledge, even to the appointed place. This took place that I might know that a man can be led by the Lord without his knowing whence and whither." (AC 1884)

Also here, Swedenborg draws a parallel with the second type of experience and the Bible, by referencing the prophet Ezekiel in the Old Testament. In several chapters Ezekiel tells how he moved in the spirit from his imprisonment in Babylon to the land of Israel, so that its miseries could become lessons and so that the hope for the future on liberation and restoration should be kept alive. The prophet tells of how a formation of fire revealed itself to him:

"He stretched out what looked like a hand and took me by the hair of my head. The Spirit lifted me up between earth and heaven and in visions of God he took me to Jerusalem, to the entrance of the north gate of the inner court, where the idol that provokes to jealousy stood." Ezek 8:3 (NIV)

These words by Ezekiel begin a whole spiritual journey of exploration, which is also the case with the following words in his fortieth chapter.

"In visions of God he took me to the land of Israel and set me on a very high mountain, on whose south side were some buildings that looked like a city." Ezek 40:2 (NIV)

As we have seen, it is clear that Swedenborg utilized personal religious criteria for his revelations. After 1758 and to his death in 1772, Swedenborg's certainty of his religious calling and his contact with a spiritual world appears only to have grown stronger. He also claimed that he had been given a unique mission and a wholly unique ability to, without difficulty, move in both worlds at the same time. When he engaged with and conversed with people, he could at the same time have conversations with beings in the spiritual world; possibly those currently with him noticed some moment of distraction in him. Sometimes he was; however, in a deeper way "in the spirit" and appears to have been so fully absorbed by the spiritual world that the natural one was disconnected.

In spite of paranormal phenomena being well recorded by contemporary writers, one looks in vain after anecdote and biographical descriptions of more commonly known paranormal phenomena in connection with Swedenborg in both his unpublished and published works. It can even be difficult for a parapsychologist to see in Swedenborg's unusual spiritual experiences the distinction between out-of-body experience and clairvoyance.

As an example of this, mention should be made of how Swedenborg on a visit to Gothenburg in 1759 tells of his experiences of a fire in the vicinity of his house at Hornsgatan in Stockholm. The description of this vision down to every detail was confirmed as to what actually had happened.[1]

On another occasion, Swedenborg helped the Dutch ambassador's widow de Marteville to find a receipt, which only her dead husband knew where it was. After some days, Swedenborg got "answers": The receipt lay in an unknown secret drawer in a writing desk on the upper floor. This was confirmed to be true.[2]

Swedenborg was undoubtedly convinced that apparent supernatural powers were active through him. However, both from religious principle and personal resentment, he avoided to do what could be perceived as miracles. These force the mind, he explained, and hence cloud the clear human sense of reason. In a real sense, he was not a friend of "the occult". With Swedenborg there are warnings against conscious attempts to contact spirits, as he meant that in this way one can be victim of deceits. He demanded respect for natural laws and wanted everything to be subject to what is truly rational.

In a small essay in Swedish in 1716, in the journal *Daedalus Hyperboreus,* Swedenborg presents the theory that human beings are constituted by a coherent system of vibrations, "tremulations". The concurrence of these, according to the author, can make possible thought-contact over great distances. In the same way, the spiritual world and its beings in our unconscious and conscious mind influence us during our whole earthly existence.

Swedenborg's Experiences and Interpretations of the Spiritual World

Swedenborg often speaks about how his inner sight has been opened, and how he, at certain times, has been admitted to the spiritual world and to the heavenly realms. Additionally, he sometimes has been able to leave his material covering to make spiritual excursions. A well

---

1   First in Immanuel Kant, *Dreams of a Spirit-seer*, 1766. Swedish edition edited by E Briem, Lund 1921, p 112, p 149. Cfr S Toksvig, *Swedenborg*, Stockholm 1949, p 199.
2   Briem ed., op.cit. p. 113, 150.

known passage in *Heaven and Hell* closely describes experiences of presence by the dying and of resurrection in such a state:

"As to the senses of the body I was brought into a state of insensibility, thus nearly into the state of the dying; but with the interior life and thought remaining unimpaired, in order that I might perceive and retain in the memory the things that happened to me, and that happen to those that are resuscitated from the dead. I perceived that the respiration of the body was almost wholly taken away; but the interior respiration of the spirit went on in connection with a slight and tacit respiration of the body. Then at first a communication of the pulse of the heart with the celestial kingdom was established, because that kingdom corresponds to the heart in man. Angels from that kingdom were seen, some at a distance, and two sitting near my head. Thus all my own affection was taken away although thought and perception continued. I was in this state for some hours. Then the spirits that were around me withdrew, thinking that I was dead; and an aromatic odor like that of an embalmed body was perceived, for when the celestial angels are present everything pertaining to the corpse is perceived as aromatic, and when spirits perceive this they cannot approach; and in this way evil spirits are kept away from man's spirit when he is being introduced into eternal life. The angels seated at my head were silent, merely sharing their thoughts with mine; and when their thoughts are received the angels know that the spirit of man is in a state in which it can be drawn forth from the body. This sharing of their thoughts was effected by looking into my face, for in this way in heaven thoughts are shared.

[3] As my thought and perception continued, that I might know and remember how resuscitation is effected, I perceived the angels first tried to ascertain what my thought was, whether it was like the thought of those who are dying, which is usually about eternal life; also that they wished to keep my mind in that thought. Afterwards I was told that the spirit of man is held in its last thought when the body expires, until it returns to the thoughts that are from its general or ruling affection in the world. Especially was I permitted to see

and feel that there was a pulling and drawing forth, as it were, of the interiors of my mind, thus of my spirit, from the body; and I was told that this is from the Lord, and that the resurrection is thus effected." (HH 449)[3]

Thus, resurrection occurs, according to Swedenborg, not on an indefinite last day in the future, but after about three days after the death of body, as the soul – or spirit – is so interwoven with the body that it cannot be entirely separated until the structure of the body begins to dissolve. According to Swedenborg spirits and angels come to meet the dying:

"The celestial angels who are with the one that is resuscitated do not withdraw from him, because they love everyone; but when the spirit comes into such a state that he can no longer be affiliated with celestial angels, he longs to get away from them. When this takes place angels from the Lord's spiritual kingdom come, through whom is given the use of light; for before this he saw nothing, but merely thought." (HH 450)

The Afterlife

In *Heaven and Hell,* Swedenborg divides life near after death into three states:

"The first state of man after death resembles his state in the world, for he is then likewise in externals, having a like face, like speech, and a like disposition, thus a like moral and civil life..." (HH 493)

It is the angels' task to tell the dead that he now is a spirit:

"The angels are extremely careful that only such ideas as savor of love shall proceed from the one resuscitated. They now tell him that he is a spirit." (HH 450)

The speech of the angels does not operate through words, but telepathically through thoughts:

"This sharing of their thoughts was effected by looking into my face, for in this way in heaven thoughts are shared." HH 449

Swedenborg has himself met dead friends:

---

3 E Swedenborg, *Heaven and Hell*, Swedish transl Baeckström, Stockholm 1944, p. 329.

"I have talked with some on the third day after their decease... to whom I mentioned that arrangements were now being made for burying their bodies; I said, for burying them; on hearing which they were smitten with a kind of surprise, saying that they were alive, and that the thing that had served them in the world was what was being buried." (HH 452)

Of the reaction of some on such confrontations, Swedenborg says:

"Those that have not believed in the world in any life of the soul after the life of the body are greatly ashamed when they find themselves to be alive." (HH 452)

Thus, not a resurrection of the mortal remains, but a direct survival of the inner man, which during the earthly life developed and acted in and through the body. Also closest after death, the spirit; however, has a human form and is recognized by earlier departed friends:

"That the spirit of man, when it has been loosed from the body, is still a man and in a like form, has been proved to me by the daily experience of many years; for I have seen such and have listened to them a thousand times, and have talked with them about this fact... nearly all that go from this world are greatly surprised to find that they are alive, and are as much men as before, with no difference whatever... The state of man's spirit that immediately follows his life in the world being such, he is then recognized by his friends and by those he had known in the world; for this is something that spirits perceive not only from one's face and speech but also from the sphere of his life when they draw near. Whenever anyone in the other life thinks about another he brings his face before him in thought, and at the same time many things of his life; and when he does this the other becomes present, as if he had been sent for or called. This is so in the spiritual world because thoughts there are shared, and there is no such space there as in the natural world. So all, as soon as they enter the other life, are recognized by their friends, their relatives, and those in any way known to them; and they talk with one another, and afterward associate in accordance with their friendships in the world." (HH 456, 494)

Memory remains:

"......he carries with him his natural memory, retaining everything that he has heard, seen, read, learned, or thought, in the world from earliest infancy even to the end of life..." (HH 461)

The senses are however sharper:

"Those that are in heaven have more exquisite senses, that is, a keener sight and hearing, and also think more wisely than when they were in the world..." (HH 462)

The surrounding after death is similar to this world, but is produced by the representations and emotions of man and made up of spiritual substances. A sensation of happiness can for example set forth a well pouring in the woods.

"This first state of man after death continues with some for days, with some for months, and with some for a year; but seldom with any one beyond a year..." (HH 498)

During *the second state* the dead begins to become accustomed to the new surroundings. What was characteristic for the first state now completely disappears, as well as that, which was created by society and tradition. Now the inner self, the true human nature, takes precedence over the outer, which is ruled by "the moral and civil laws of life" and emerges to the second state and that environment:

"When the spirit is in the state of his interiors it becomes clearly evident what the man was in himself when he was in the world, for at such times he acts from what is his own. He that had been in the world interiorly in good then acts rationally and wisely, and even more wisely than in the world, because he is released from connection with the body, and thus from those earthly things that caused obscurity and interposed as it were a cloud. But he that was in evil in the world, then acts foolishly and insanely, and even more insanely than in the world, because he is free and under no restraint." (HH 505)

The human spirit thus gradually chooses the environment in the other world where it feels connection and inner enjoyment. Thus, if one does not enjoy the presence of the highest angels, the celestial, one is instead associated with the angels in the degree below, the spiritual, and if one does not feel well with them either, one is conjoined to "the good spirits". If also these lack inner congruence he is drawn by an inner force to societies of lower spirits, to those who are spiritually the same and are his likes and soul mates. But to all, death must, according to Swedenborg, mean the gateway to a happier state, to a life in more inner freedom, than is possible in the material world. Kind and friendly spiritual beings stand on the other side to take care of each and everyone and mildly lead them to their spiritual home in the other world, which already now exists in his or her innermost being. First, as we have seen, the spirit arrives at the middle world, the world of spirits, where one's inner self is examined. During the later stages there is talk about heaven and hells but never with reference to places for reward or punishment. Children and unaccomplished people get further education in a loving community with angels.

During the third state, spirits are prepared through teaching for their entry into the heavenly realm.
Angels instruct via thoughts. The spirits, who, because of their inner state, have removed themselves to hellish states, cannot be reached by teaching in the third state."When spirits have been prepared for heaven by instruction, they are clothed with angelic garments, which are mostly glowing white as if made of fine linen; and they are thus brought to the way that leads upwards towards heaven, and are delivered there to angel guards, and afterwards are received by other angels and introduced into societies and into much blessedness there." (HH 519)

Such passages through various states as described by Swedenborg remind us, as C G Jung has noted, of the *Tibetan Book of the Dead.* Also, here spirits on the other side must tell the dead one that he really is dead, and he is thereby helped to pass along.[4]

---

4 W Y Evans-Wentz, *The Tibetan Book of the Dead,* Bergh, Stockholm – Malmö 1974, p. 54.

Comparison between Swedenborg's Experiences and Moody's Material

It is perhaps difficult to see Swedenborg's distinctions between different kinds of spiritual experiences. His experiences primarily served as a confirmation of the new vision of the spiritual world that he felt a Divine calling to set forth. He says that he is describing the other world "ex auditis et visis", "according to what has been heard and seen", but it can often be difficult to separate real experiences from symbolic presentations. There is reason; however, to try to compare Moody's ideal type[5] with Swedenborg, whose experiences of our passage to the other world is similar and definitely reminds us of Moody's recorded material.

"An unpleasant sound, a high ringing or vibrating sound is heard..."

Experiences followed by such phenomena, Swedenborg talks of in connection with his two perhaps most important experiences: how his inner sight was opened to the other world, one in the Easter of 1744 and the second in April, 1745. The first is described in Swedenborg's *Dream diary*. Here Swedenborg tells of how after having gone to bed at around ten in the evening, he gets repeated bouts of shaking, starting from the from the head through the whole body, in combinations with a roaring sound. At the same time, he feels that "something holy" comes over him. He goes to sleep, but shortly after midnight a new attack occurs, "with a crashing sound as if many weathers collided together." "When I was cast down in that moment I was fully awake and saw I was cast down, wondered what it could mean and talked as if I was awake, but found that the words were put in my mouth."[6]

This is told in connection with a highly realistic vision of Christ, which can be compared, according to his close friends, to what he

5 Moody's ideal type is found in *Medvetandet och döden,*
    eds. K Wistrand och J Pilotti Stockholm 1982, kap 8. p 113.

6 See *Swedenborg's Dreams*, Knut Barr's edition, Stockholm 1924, p. 24.

had experienced the following year in London. He also remembers similar sound experiences and also experiences of seeing light.

"... and she suddenly gets a feeling of that she moves trough a dark tunnel..."

Such experiences Swedenborg can very well have experienced, but not wanted to record. He has recorded many things about tunnels, cavities and caves in the other world, but they mostly relate to experiences of "infernal" realms or "hells", and to negative experiences there – here undoubtedly symbolism plays a role in Swedenborg's images from the spiritual world.

"...Thereafter she suddenly is out of her physical body..."

Swedenborg claims that he has gone through the early stages of death. He experiences states of separating, and a drawing out or loosening of the spirit from the body. He compares this with the Apostle Paul's elevation to "the third heaven". In this state, Swedenborg says, it appears as if "the soul elevates itself as if it was free from the body. "It leaves the body, and if it remains there the connection is broken between body and soul. The human being is a spirit clothed in a body. The out-of-body state is called by him "to be in the spirit". He was often "in the spirit". This state was combined, according to his statements at various times, with the ceasing of the bodily breathing or with a state of what he called "the inner breathing".

Ernst Arbman, in his great work of psychology of religions, *Ecstasy and Religious Trance*,[7] also describes Swedenborg and shows with some reliable examples of how eyewitnesses have experienced Swedenborg's actions during and after his trance, when he seemed disconnected from the normal world.

---

7   E Arbman, *Ecstasy or Religious Trance*, Uppsala 1963.

*"... but still in the immediate physical environment and
sees her body in a distance as if she was only a spectator..."*
Such cases are rare in Swedenborg, and it is uncertain if there is a
clear parallel. Some relations in the stories of others, of how Swedenborg or other persons, according to Swedenborg, see "the double of himself", play; however, a significant role as motifs in August
Strindberg's *Occult Diary."*

**".... She collects herself after awhile.... And notices that
she has a "body" of a different nature and with completely
other abilities than the one she has left behind."**
Swedenborg experiences this state in the following way:

"All his senses are as fully awake as in the highest wakefulness of
the body; the sight, the hearing, and, wonderful to say, the touch,
which is then more exquisite than it can ever be in the wakefulness
of the body. In this state also spirits and angels have been seen
to the very life, and also heard, and, wonderful to say, have been
touched, and almost nothing of the body then intervened." (AC
1883)

Here, Swedenborg points out that sight as well as other senses are
sharpened. He also mentions touch, not present in Moody's material.

He also points out that the dead person may not always understand that he is dead but has to have this shown to him, as the
first state is similar to earthly existence. The dead person lives in his
unconscious, one could say.

**"...Other beings come to meet and help her. She sees a
glimpse of the spirits of relatives and friends who have
died before her..."**
Also, we recognize this from Swedenborg, who pointed out that spirits and angels approached him when he was in the spirit and also
met with deceased friends, among them the engineer Christopher

Polhem.[8] The angels said that the dead person was a spirit and taught him about his new existence.

In the work *Apocalypisis Revelata*, Swedenborg says: "Once on waking from sleep, I fell into a profound meditation concerning God; and when I looked up, I saw above me in heaven a very bright light in an oval form; and when I fixed my attention on that light, it receded to the sides, and entered into the circumference. And then behold, heaven was opened to me, and I saw some magnificent things, and angels standing in the form of a circle on the southern side of the opening, speaking with one another. And because I was enkindled with the desire of hearing what they were saying, it was therefore given me first to hear the sound, which was full of heavenly love, and afterwards their speech, which was full of wisdom from that love." (AR 961)[9]

Swedenborg often mentions luminous phenomena associated with his light experiences. The discussion in Religious psychology on photisms, that is on luminous phenomena, in Swedenborg, is thoroughly discussed in the above mentioned study by Arbman.

Swedenborg himself says:

"That there is light in the heavens those who think from nature alone cannot comprehend; and yet such is the light in the heavens that it exceeds by many degrees the noon-day light of the world... The brightness and splendor of the light of heaven are such as cannot be described." (HH 126)[10]

"The light of heaven is not a natural light, like the light of the world, but a spiritual light." (HH 127)[11]

The light stands for divine truth and wisdom - and love. The ang-

---

8   E Swedenborg, *Diarium Spirituale* IV. Ed. by I Tafel, London och Stuttgart 1845, p. 65.

9   E Swedenborg, *Apocalypsis Revelata*, vol 2. Swedish transl Manby, Stockholm 1918, p. 504.

10   E Swedenborg, *Heaven and Hell*, nr 126 och 127. A.s. p. 90.

11   Ibid. nr 131 och 133, pp. 94-95.

90

els are beings of light. Swedenborg's view of light, as love and wisdom concurs in a remarkable way with the experiences of patients in recent clinical material.

Swedenborg's Death

Swedenborg's life appears to have ended truly peacefully and harmoniously with the craftsman's family, Shearsmith, in London. There are several witnesses that said he experienced a call from the other world to come over there at a certain moment. Shearsmith's housemaid, Elisabeth Reynolds, is to have heard him, some days in advance, to predict the time of his passing. She said that based on his mental state: "He was as glad as if he had been given leave or going out to have a good time."

In the headquarters of the English Methodists there was a certain commotion about a small short letter from Swedenborg, where he wanted only to report that he could not, as he had wished, meet anyone on the 29th of March 1772, since he then would pass to the other world. This happened just as he had foretold.

All indications are that Swedenborg's own departure was joined to a luminous and peaceful experience that higher beings were calling him over to them, in order to pass to new tasks in a spiritual world.

Notes:

1. D Ottoson, *Nervsystemets fysiologi*. Natur och Kultur, Stockholm 1978, p 224.
2. E Swedenborg, *De Fibra* and the third unpublished part of *Oeconomia regni animalis* ("On the Nerve"), 1741-42. Ed. by JJG Wilkinson, London 1847, p 243.
3. E Swedenborg, *Angelic Wisdom on Divine Love and Wisdom* nr 391, Sw transl by Sevén-Lind, Stockholm 1926, p 272.
4. E Swedenborg, *Arcana Coelestia* (Heavenly Secrets) nr. 1882, vol. 3 Sw transl Sevén, Kristianstad 1866, p 314.
5. AC nr 1883.
6. AC nr. 1884.
7. First in Immanuel Kant, *Dreams of a Spirit-seer*, 1766. Swedish edition edited by E Briem, Lund 1921, p 112, p 149. Cfr S Toksvig, *Swedenborg*, Stockholm 1949, p 199.
8. Briem ed., op.cit. p 113, 150.
9. E Swedenborg, *Heaven and Hell*, Swedish transl Baeckström, Stockholm 1944, p 329.
10. W Y Evans-Wentz, *The Tibetan Book of the Dead*, Bergh, Stockholm – Malmö 1974, p 54.
11. Moody's ideal type is found in *Medvetandet och döden*, eds. K Wistrand och J Pilotti Stockholm 1982, kap 8. p 113.
12. See *Swedenborg's Dreams*, Knut Barr's edition, Stockholm 1924, p 24.
13. E Arbman, *Ecstasy or Religious Trance*, Uppsala 1963.
14. E Swedenborg, *Diarium Spirituale* IV. Ed. by I Tafel, London och Stuttgart 1845, p 65.
15. E Swedenborg, *Apocalypsis Revelata*, vol 2. Swedish transl Manby, Stockholm 1918, p 504.
16. E Swedenborg, *Heaven and Hell*, nr 126 och 127. A.s. p 90.
17. Ibid. nr 131 och 133, pp 94-95.

SWEDENBORG IN STOCKHOLM[1]

Olle Hjern

We know that Emanuel Swedenborg, spent a large portion of his time traveling through countries outside Sweden and that he passed the last part of his life in England. However, it is quite clear that the place where he worked the most and where he returned again and again was Stockholm, the place of his birth. Of course this city has changed dramatically since the time when he lived there, but the whole structure of the central areas, where he was reportedly seen by many, is still largely the same as it was in his lifetime.

According to the "old calendar"[2] Emanuel Swedenborg was born on January 29, 1688 in Stockholm in the parish of Jacobs Kyrka, on Regeringsgatan 18, in the center of the present city, and the distance from there to the old royal palace was quite short. The entries of the baptism of the child Emanuel Swedenborg are still preserved in the parish church.[3] His father served as a royal court and army chaplain. In the park that is there is the Kungsträdgården (Royal Garden), and we also have reports about it of how later the adult Emanuel had met with people in this central Stockholm park. Opposite the park today is Jernkontoret, the "Iron Office," which today holds certain functions of the Bergs Collegium of the eighteenth-century. The Bergs Collegium was dissolved in the mid-nineteenth-century, but its activity is carried on by the Kommers Kollegium (Chamber of Commerce) and Jern Kontoret, both of which existed previously.

On the outer side of the corner of the Jern Kontoret building can be seen a large portrait medallion of Emanuel Swedenborg, and various other eminent scientists. Around 1950, when I was a young man and new in the New Church, we used to explore the building on Regeringsgatan to find out how much of the house is left from the time when Swedenborg was born. A significant part of the house was still standing, but some years later, all the buildings around the

St. Jacobs Kyrka were torn down, and now there are only recently erected buildings.

It seems about the same was the case with the house in the vicinity of the nearly vanished Brunkebergstorg, where Swedenborg's first permanent residence in Stockholm was as an adult. It was only when he had reached the mature age of thirty-six years and held a secure position as a full assessor of the Bergs Collegium (July 15, 1724) that he rented his own premises in the house of Count Gyllenborg in the parish of Sancta Clara, not far from today's central station. It is said that during his stay in this mansion he had a servant, named Olof. At that time he also had a close if not always cordial relationship with Lars Benzelstierna, who was married to his sister Hedvig and lived in the same house.[4]

The island of Gamla Stan (Old Town) is the very center of Stockholm, and Emanuel worked and lived there for a long time. The Bergs Collegium in Swedenborg's time had its seat at the Mynttorget in Gamla Stan in a building that was used until recently by the Swedish central government. When the Bergs Collegium moved away from the Mynttorget, parts of Swedenborg's furniture were moved into the building in Riddarholmen which is occupied at the present day by the Kommers Kollegium.

The Kommers Kollegium is located near the Riddarholms Church, the royal burial church, where all the royal friends of Swedenborg were buried. Quite near it is the Riddarhuset (Knights House or House of Nobles), where he represented his family from 1719 until his last years as a very active member of the Parliament. In Emanuel's childhood the old royal palace, which was also in this region, was destroyed by a fire, and as he was growing up the new palace, which can be seen today, was built by the great Swedish architect Nicodemus Tessin and was completed by his son Carl Gustaf Tessin, a close friend of Swedenborg.

Swedenborg's sister Hedvig died in 1728 and shortly thereafter he withdrew from the northern part of the city center to Gamla Stan. He moved his quarters to Stora Nygatan, today No. 7, at the corner of Stora Nygatan and Göran Helsing Gränd. His residence there was very close to the Bergs Collegium, which is now located at the Mynttorget, and during the five years he spent there, he completed his three-volume work *Philosophica Opera et Mineralia.* He recorded an impressive vision of the Stora Nygatan in his *Spiritual Diary:*

My inward sight was opened and I looked into Stockholm's Stora Nygatan[5] and then saw many walking there. Next I was led onto the street. And there were angels with me. They said that in the houses roundabout no one was alive but all were dead, that is to say, spiritually, so that they were horrified and did not want to go further. When they are dead in the houses there, then no windows appear in the houses, but holes, inside which all is dark; but when they are alive, windows appear and in them people. I then was led to Lilla Nygatan.[6] There, it was said, a few were alive. Then I was lead back toward Slussen. At the market place there scarcely anyone was alive. Where the food shops were it was said there were few. Likewise on the other side of the bridge, where food shops around the market-place were, there were not any who were alive, except in one house, on the corner. There was no one in the great houses there besides this. Then, on the long street from the marketplace, where the pharmacy was, there was also no one alive, but I did not look far. And not a living spirit was seen from the marketplace toward the sea, and then farther. *(Spiritual Experiences* 5711)

Swedenborg's experience in assessing the people in the spiritual world in this part of Stockholm is an accurate physical picture of this district today. The same streets – Stora Gatan, Lilla Nygatan and Långgatan – are still here, as well as the marketplace near the water, the Kornhamnstorg.

When Swedenborg returned from his fourth trip abroad in 1740, he fell in love with this street and rented an apartment left vacant by one of his relatives, the great scientist Carl von Linné. It was located in the so-called Räntmästarehuset at the corner of Slussplan Skeppsbron and in the southern part of Gamla Stan, near the water, which separates this part of the south-central part of Stockholm, Södermalm. The old buildings there are maintained more or less as at Swedenborg's time.[7]

In November 1740 Linnaeus invited Swedenborg, to join the recently created Academy of Sciences, and they must have known each other pretty well. Swedenborg's older cousin Johan Moraeus served in Emanuel's home as his private teacher when he was still a student of medicine.[8] He and his wife took over the family estate Sveden near Falun in Dalarna, and that is the reason why Linnaeus and Moraeus' daughter, Sara Elizabeth Moraea, was married there. During the years 1738 to 1740 Linnaeus was active as a physician in Gamla Stan, and he held very populär lectures there.[9] Swedenborg and Linnaeus could not at all avoid meeting. It is quite likely that they saw each other every day.

A volume of the original edition of the work *Heaven and Hell*, Swedenborg gave to Linnaeus has been preserved by the Library of the Swedish Academy of Sciences and is now in the University Library of Stockholm.

Swedenborg was quite often abroad, including 1743-1745, but during that time he had apartments that were prepared for him in Stockholm. In 1745 he was again in the Räntmästarehuset residence. Frans G. Lindh, the principal researcher on Swedenborg Swedenborg's locations in Stockholm describes the residence as follows:

According to the tax list the first-floor apartment was down to the south, because, as is well known, Swedenborg preferred to have his home in rooms that receive sun from the south. Downstairs was a café that was certainly visited by the coffee-lover Swedenborg and that was in possession of the shop-keeper with the Danish-sounding name Finn Holsten Hobel.[10]

From the report of a Swedish clergyman, we also know that Emanuel Swedenborg could be found now and then in the Taverne Gyldene Freden, the "The Golden Peace," a restaurant of that time which still exists today in Gamla Stan. In the eighteenth century this place especially connected with the local appearance of the National Swedish poet Carl Michael Bellman, who was famous as a singer and musician. Bellman was younger than Swedenborg, but somewhat his contemporary. Obviously both of them had good contacts with the family of the Dutch Ambassador de Marteville, and both had problems in connection with the same Archbishop Peter Filenius.[11] They had their residence close together in the south of Stockholm,[12] and it is likely that Bellman and Swedenborg, two well known personalities and Stockholm compatriots, saw each other now and then.

The name of the clergyman, to whom we owe this information, was Carl Nyrén, who wrote:

To celebrate his appointment, a week after the event Bishop Filenius asked me to serve as master of ceremonies on that occasion and to drive around in a rented wagon and invite guests to the Gyldene Freden inn, where they were treated courteously. Among other acquaintances I had those of Assessor Swedenborg, deeply revered by some people, while others made fun of him. He was not very talkative, and went away after the first toasts were brought out.[13]

Not too far from the center of Stockholm lies the property Svindersvik and the Drottningholm Palace, which are both very clean and well maintained and regularly shown to the public. In Svindersvik Swedenborg took part in the social evenings, which were arranged by his friend Carl Gustaf Tessin. And on one occasion it is reported that instead of the usual billiard game the guests remained seated a long time to listen to Swedenborg, who gave an overview of the best part of his ideas.[14] This was quite obviously in the year that Swedenborg's role as a seer and prophet and as the author of the anonymously published religious works became generally known.

The name Drottningholm derives from Drottning, "the Queen" – and in Sweden we associate this palace especially with Queen Lovisa Ulrika, a strong, intelligent but contradictory woman. She received the palace as a personal gift, although it was named after a former queen. She sent after Swedenborg to inquire after her deceased brother, who was in another world. She must have made a strong impression on Swedenborg, and he had probably visited Drottningholm several times.[15] He told C. C. Gjörwell in August 1764, that he had just handed recently printed books in England to the king and queen at Drottningholm and was received favorably.[16] I have seen one of these volumes with a beautiful mark of the queen in the collection of the present day royal library in Stockholm. Several more volumes of this type were once quite obviously this library, but since the library had duplicates, in the nineteenth century some there were sold at auctions, likely to libraries and individuals in England and America.

Currently, the Drottningholm Palace with its beautiful park is the permanent residence of the royal family, and it is also well known for its interesting Royal Theatre, where in the summer, operas and ballets of the eighteenth-century are listed. The theater dates from Swedenborg's time, and then it was only for royal guests. One can speculate if Swedenborg had ever been there.

In 1743 Swedenborg bought a part of the block Mullvaden Första in Södermalm, and later he took up the Hornsgatan residence (today no. 41- 43).

Södermalm, the southern part of today's city center, has changed quite a bit, and in the biographies of Swedenborg we are reminded of large and destructive fires in this district, especially the one that he saw in a vision in 1759 in Gothenburg.[17] Nonetheless the streets and many buildings from Swedenborg's time remain. On Hornsgatan is the Mary Magdalene Church, which Swedenborg occasionally visited. It was severely damaged by fire, but restored again. There Swedenborg led a famous 1751 interview with Christopher Polhem on the occasion of Polhem's funeral, in which Polhem expressed his astonishment at the pastors address regarding Polhem's future resurrection, since he had already risen and was fully alive *(Spiritual Experiences* 4752). Near this church you can still find an old place now called Mariatorget, the former Adolf Fredrik's Torg. In his later years Swedenborg lived near this place, and it is not so long ago that the Stockholm city authorities honored Swedenborg by establishing a Swedenborg Park and set up a bust of Swedenborg created by one of Stockholm's sculptors, Gustav Nordahl. At its base there is a scene in relief in, which Swedenborg s in his nearby garden introduces a little girl to an angel by letting her look in a mirror.[18]

The Mariatorget is located in the vicinity of today's Swedenborgsgatan (Swedenborg Street), and consequently the place of his former property. In that part of the block at the Mullvaden on Krukmakargatan in which Swedenborg lived, is a recently built house where the architect Nils Orento has tried to restore parts of Swedenborg's garden. The gate to his garden is wrought-iron, the creation of the young Stockholm wrought-iron craftswoman Annika Söderström, and it contains figures of plants from Swedenborg's garden. Below that grows the pea, which was apparently imported together with other seeds from America, where the family Svedberg-Swedenborg maintained so many contacts.[19]

We do not know exactly when he moved into his own house, but we know that he lived there in 1747, when he at his own request, he received permission from the king to withdraw from his office in the Bergs Collegium.[20] At least he now had his own house, surrounded by a large and beautiful garden with "summer houses," where he could open his spirit in quiet harmony to the divine revelations granted to him, and which he felt himself obliged to share with the world. Rev. C. J. N. Manby, pastor of the New Church in Stockholm until his death in 1920, wrote in a publication:

We'll never forget to our deep spiritual reverence, when in 1865 for the first time we entered the place at Hornsgatan in Stockholm where Swedenborg had his home during the last decades of his life. The house was still in good condition. The garden was quite large, leaving a free space around the house. A gate or a trellis door formed the entrance to a long path; at its end was the well known summerhouse. We entered his house and learned how a gentleman in the Eighteenth Century lived. We climbed the stairs to the upper floor. His summer home was kept in pretty good condition. We put our names in a register that was put out there for this purpose. We also climbed into the attic of the summer house. Everything was so new to us. It was a lovely summer day. No wonder our feelings were full of sacred awe.[21]

Cyriel Sigstedt quoted a description of Swedenborgs summer home in her biography, from an article from 1867 in the English between *Intellectual Repository:*

At the end of the walk are two poplars; behind them is the summerhouse, which looks down the garden walk between the trees. It occupies the middle of the end of the garden and is about fourteen feet square. There are three stone steps up to the doorsill, a double door, on each side a window; a vine gathers over them and the top of the door, and clambers partly over the roof. On the two sides are external traces, and the shutters, of windows which are now obliterated inside. In the room is another door opposite the entrance; it opens into a lobby, a pace wide, on the right of which is a cupboard, on the left the bricked-up doorway, which formerly led to the covered way; a part of it remains between the summer-house and the long side of the garden, away from the street. From that angle to within a few yards of the house the covered way has been removed. It appears as if it originally ran down the length of the garden, and served as a protected path to the summerhouse-pleasant in bad weather or at night. Like the house, the summerhouse or study is built of logs, raised on a granite foundation about a couple of feet from the ground. It is as gay in color as the house – dark red lines on yellow ground, with white window frames and a black roof, all well contrasted with the bright green of the vine. The roof does not go up to a ridge or gable, but is broken through by a short vertical portion, in which are long narrow windows, serving to lightthe loft over the room. This, in turn, is roofed with hip rafters. On the two points of the ridge is a ball ornament, on which is perched a little golden star. A chair which belonged to Swedenborg remains in the summer-house. His organ lately stood there, but has passed into the possession of Mr. Hammer, in whose museum, in Byström's Villa, it may be seen.[22]

Christian Hammer, the former owner of the organ, was a well-known jeweler and collector in Stockholm, and very interested Swedenborg. In particular, he served as a model for "the wealthy blind man" in August Strindberg's *Dream Play*. The Nordiska Museet and Skansen bought the organ from his estate.[23]

F. G. Lindh wrote about Swedenborg's home in his artide "Swedenborg som Söderbo":

Alongside Hornsgatan were only farmhouses, on the western corner of the property was a carriage house with the associated storage space for garden equipment, and on the eastern corner there was a barn and cattle shed, which on the side facing the court was connected with a log house. On its ground floor were three large rooms, one of the two was undoubtedly a spacious kitchen, and there was a room upstairs. Most likely his gardener and his family lived there. They also looked after his horses and cows. It can be assumed with certainty that he did not let the buildings that were equipped for the livestock stand empty, especially since it was known that Swedenborg loved to mingle with the society, both in town and in the country, and therefore needed ways to get around comfortably. He probably had a horse carriage. It is also known with certainty, that Stockholmers of that time generally kept cows that grazed during the day on the commons outside the city and in the evening were driven home to their stables by special, so-called cowherds. Milk was also an important, if not the most important nutritional element in Swedenborg's diet. The fact that he lived so far outside in Södermalm was certainly an advantage for him, as his cows were not so long a way to and from the pastures outside the city. On the back of the gardener's cottage on the property out there was a small garden with flower beds and shrubs in boxes, which were trimmed in the Dutch way in the forms of birds, pots and all sorts of other shapes. On the other side of this small landscaped courtyard across from the gardener's house, was Swedenborg's own abode, a house half of logs and [half] of brick, paneled on the inside and outside. Swedenborg's house was painted yellow, and the gardener's house red; and both were on solid stone foundations. On the ground floor Swedenborg had two wide rooms and one small room. One of the large rooms was probably used as a reception room or parlor, the other as a writing room, and the little one was probably used as a bedroom. The upper floor of the living quarters had been prepared as a sort of greenhouse, probably having a glass wall to the south and with a brick floor. The greenhouse and the living quarters below were well-equipped with stoves. Clearly the house was warm and comfortable in the severe cold of winter; Swedenborg constantly used to burn a wood fire in the writing room. It could be cold sitting and writing all day; and the fact that Swedenborg suffered from a digestive disorder, and had to live almost exclusively on a milk diet was probably due to his sedentary lifestyle. On the other hand it is known that he allowed no wood fire in his bedroom, but instead used all the more linen and quilts at night. This was a habit he had adopted on his trips abroad, notably England and France, where, as Swedenborg was always very much in interested trees, shrubs and flowers and no doubt, like the people of the Ancient Church elders he described, perceived these growing things as representing and symbolizing spiritual realities. In this home for several years and with tremendous diligence he now wrote the volumes that contain what he saw as the revelation of the Lord for the New Church. To the world outside he seemed to have led a quiet and secluded life, although he was always ready to welcome those who would like to visit him. Around 1760 he had three female servants and a few years later, we hear for the first time that a family took care of his garden and he came to enjoy its produce. Anecdotes fairly accurately testify to all of the great affection which the servants felt for their master.[25]

Swedenborg's close friend Carl Robsahm, who lived in another property in Stockholm near Swedenborg, in his memoirs about Swedenborg tells us of how worried the gardener and his wife were when Swedenborg seemed to be in a state of great bewilderment and despair during certain nights.[26] From his room they could hear words like, "Lord, help me! Oh Lord, my God, forsake me not! "But when they approached him, he calmly assured them, that everything was alright with him and that whatever would happen to him, would happen with the Lord's permission. The gardeners wife also told Robsahm how frightened she had been, when she once opened the door of Swedenborg's room and then seen his "burning eyes". But Swedenborg said to her." Fear not, the Lord has opened my bodily eyes and I saw in the spirit [in *spiritu]*, but in a moment I will have recovered and I am not injured."[27] After half an hour, she told Robsahm, this appearance, which was like fire, had disappeared.

The garden is mentioned particularly in connection with another event of the year 1769, when a process was initiated by the estate of the clergy of the Parliament to admit Emanuel Swedenborg to a mental hospital – a very common method of the time to deal with religious dissidents.

One of his friends in the parliament had heard of the plan and sent him a message that he should leave the country immediately. But Swedenborg remained. Robsahm tells us: "Swedenborg was very sad, and then he soon came out into his garden, where he knelt and prayed to the Lord in tears, asking what he should do now? And he received the comforting conviction that no harm would befall him"[28] The plans were not implemented, at that time Swedenborg had highly placed advocates in the country.[29]

The orthodox clergy were harsh and judgmental, but due to the influence of the writings of the philosopher Christian Wolff, whose philosophy of interest to Swedenborg too, some important ministers were more moderate.

One of these men who could have helped Swedenborg in this difficult situation was Andrew Knös. In this regard I would like to quote from a well-informed book of the Swedish scholar, Dr. H. I. Carlson:

When there was a discussion of Swedenborg's writings within the clerical estate at the parliament in 1769 with the purpose of declaring that their author is sick and if possible would be brought to an institution, one of the most learned and orthodox members of the class of, Dean Andreas Knös was tasked to deliver a verdict in the matter, and this man, who was conscientious, not to judge what he did not know thoroughly, began a serious and impartial study of all these extensive works, the consequence of which was that he finally was convinced of their truth. The state then decided to discontinue the proceedings and the matter was allowed to rest.[30]

Andreas Knös died in 1799 as a fully committed believer of the New Church.[31]

We have a description of a visit to Swedenborgs garden in the book *Notes in Swedish History* printed by Carl Christopher Gjörwell in 1786 in Stockholm. As librarian of the Royal Library in Stockholm Gjörwell visited Swedenborg on 28 August 1764 to obtain his recently published books for the library and also to investigate his ideas about religion. After his visit there Gjörwell wrote:

I recently came back from Assessor Emanuel Swedenborg, whom on behalf of the Royal Library I asked about his works last published in Holland. I met him dressed in plain clothes as he cared for his plants in the garden which he has next to his house in Södermalm on Hornsgatan. His residence was a wooden house, low, and it looked like a garden pavilion, and the windows looked out onto the garden. Without his knowing me and without knowing of my request, he said with a smile on my face. "You are taking a walk here in the garden" I told him then that I wanted to have the honor to visit him on behalf of the Royal Library, to ask him about some of his latest works, so that we could have a complete collection of his works, because we already own the earlier volumes that he had handed over to the Royal secretary, Mr. Wile. "Yes, with the greatest pleasure," was his answer. "We already intended to send them there" he added, "since the reason for me publishing them was that they might become generally known and come into possession of intelligent people." I thanked him for his courtesy, and he showed me the books. And then we walked around the garden. Despite the fact that he is an old man and the gray hairs stuck out everywhere from under his wig, he walked briskly, spöke withjoy and with particular glee. His face was thin and quite skinny but cheerful and smiling. On his own initiative he soon started to talk about his ideas, and since hearing this with my own ears was, in fact, the second purpose of my visit, I listened very eagerly to what he said and did not contradict his teachings, but did no more than readily put forth questions, as if it would serve my own enlightenment.[32]

The report on another remarkable visit to Swedenborg's garden can be found in the book *Tessin and Tessiniana* (Tessin and Memorabilia), published in Stockholm in 1819, with excerpts from Carl Gustaf Tessin's diaries and manuscripts. Like Gjörwell, Tessin also went there to learn more about Swedenborg's visions and his teachings. He was well received, and Tessin mentions his happy, cheerful and friendly, jovial and open attitude. He generously gave Tessin information and promised to send him a copy of *Heaven and Hell*. This visit took place in March 1760.[33]

Robsahm mentioned three summer houses in Swedenborg's garden, one with rather strange doors, a maze ("just to amuse respectable people ... and their children"), and a blind door that opened and by a mirror on the other side gave the illusion of a much larger garden. Of course that was the door that he opened in the probably true anecdote when he wanted to show the young girl Greta Askbom an angel. All the stories about the man give evidence of a happy nature, playfulness and a great love for children.

It was also claimed that shortly after Swedenborg's death his actual house had been destroyed for fear of local spirits.[34] But there is little doubt that Rev. C. J. N. Manby had visited the right house, the house where Emanuel lived and worked regularly. This house had a connecting passage, a corridor, to the still preserved summer house. It was said that in his work he was surrounded mainly by biblical texts in Latin and the original languages, dictionaries, and his own manuscripts and excerpts from the Bible, and probably also by his record of his own spiritual experience. Consequently when it was not too cold, he must have worked quite often in the summer house.

As a staff Swedenborg often had married couples. Then the husband obviously cared for the horses, cows and the garden, from which he could generally use some of the produce, while the wife took the necessary care of Swedenborg's household. F. G. Lindh has observed

– and his sources were the census records of the City of Stockholm – that these servants did remarkably well in their retirement. When Swedenborg eventually moved into his house on the Hornsgatan, the couple had their three girls between ten and fifteen years living with them.[35]

There were different stories told about Swedenborg's life during his later years in the south of Stockholm. From these years, we have to accept a report of his hesitation to partake of the Lord's Supper in the parish of his domicile, the municipality of Maria Magdalena. It is needs to be mentioned that for a long time it had been a matter of national duty in the state church of Sweden to take this sacrament. It is said that he had spoken to two bishops on the matter. Swedenborg claimed that he lived in conjunction with the Lord and the spiritual world and that that was enough for him and he could not stand the preaching of the pastor. But he agreed to accept the sacrament from his curate, for whom he felt a greater spiritual friendship.[36]

From Swedenborg's last years of life we have reports of visits of rather young men, all of whom were seriously interested in spiritual things. One of them was obviously the visionary "Skara boy," whom Swedenborg's friend Gabriel Beyer in Gothenburg thought that would be able to reveal healing treatments from the spiritual world. Swedenborg confirmed that the experiences of the boy testified to contacts with the spiritual world, but at the same time he stressed his immaturity both in terms of age and with respect to spirituality. Yet he was very interested in the boy. He asked that he be sent to him in Stockholm and promised to arrange that he would be cared for properly.[37]

An oral but quite probable tradition is that Swedenborg was visited by the young Jonas Pehrson Odhner, who was a private teacher in one of the first families of the New Church in Sweden, the family of Lars Lindström, who were personally well-acquainted with Swedenborg. In 1795 in Copenhagen Odhner published the first Swedish translation of *The True Christian Religion*. He was one of the clergymen of the Lutheran Swedish Church.[38]

Two fairly well-known Swedish clergymen were also among Swedenborg's visitors at Hornsgatan. Both were probably not very fond of the Lutheran orthodoxy. Both two at the time of their visit appear to have been in very good agreement with Swedenborg in spiritual matters. One of the two was Nicolas Collin, who had been active during the long period in which Jesper Svedberg and his many "heresies" dominated the Swedish Church in America. On his visit Collin first interest was understandably information about his recently deceased brother. Swedenborg gave him no such information, but he invited him into the house for coffee, and the two gentlemen discussed the problem of the human soul and the concept of the spiritual world. Among other things, they considered the ideas in Wallerius *Psychologia Empirica,* published in 1755 in Stockholm.[39] The other notable cleric was Andreas Rutström, author of hymns, principals and at that time a central figure among the Moravians in Sweden. This man remained in exile for several years on account of heresy and in 1772 was in jail in Sweden. Swedenborg said to Carl Robsahm that "this Rutström saw everything, but his life and his deeds showed that his Moravian sect, in which he had long ago been confirmed, even to persuasion, was dearest to him.[40]

In Swedenborg's biographies oral traditions are recorded about personal contacts between Swedenborg and the most noteworthy central figure in the early New Church movement in Sweden, Christian Johansén, a pious and devoted husband, a true spiritual leader. His correspondence in spiritual matters left its mark on a large part of the New Church movement in Sweden. Copies of his letters were widely dispersed, and in some Swedish archives, there are large collections of copied letters from him. He began his studies of Swedenborg in 1767 at the young age of twenty-one. He was also a pioneer of the Swedish iron industry and technology. The biggest day of his life, mentioned almost everywhere in his numerous letters but recently found documented in a note in a preserved personal diary, was a beautiful winter day in Stockholm, where the snow fell all day. On January 3rd, 1770 he welcomed Swedenborg into his home. The meeting appears to have given Johansén significantly renewed encouragement as a believer in the New Church. It is possible that on this day they had spoken about the work *De Cultu et Amore Dei.* It was often said in the tradition of the New Church that Swedenborg told Johansen that this work is of lesser importance than the later works. But Johansen felt that it was nevertheless of great value and soon after he began the translating it into Swedish. His translation of the manuscript is preserved in the Royal Library in Stockholm (Doc. II, 709, 710).[41]

The Swedish author Carl-Göran Ekerwald writes in a new artide on Swedenborg:

One of the younger friends of Swedenborg was the chemist Carl Wilhelm Scheele, the discoverer of oxygen. As Swedenborg planned his last trip—I think it was 1770 to Holland and England—he decided that the remaining goods and chattel of Hornsgatan should go to Scheele, who at the time worked in the pharmacy with the name of Korpen [The Raven].[42]

However, at the same time Swedenborg had ordered that a marble table with inlaid cards, along with five small pictures inlaid with bird motifs, be handed over to his earlier workplace in Mynttorget in Stockholm. They can still be seen in the premises of the Swedish Kommers Kollegium (Commerce). In 1763 Swedenborg wrote, a trea ti se "Huru inläggningar ske uti marble skifvor til bord cast eller annan hus-zirat" (How to make inlays in marble slabs or other household decorations), which was published in the annual yearbook of the Royal Swedish Academy of Sciences. Of course, the marble table and other objects were not made by Swedenborg himself, but ordered by him and then manufactured under his supervision in Holland.[43]

After his death Swedenborg's residence in the south of Stockholm imderwent many changes. Some parts were torn down or cut back, other parts soon gutted. In the 1880s it was somewhat uncertain what was authentically "Swedenborgian."[44] The part that was undeniably authentic was the small *Lusthus* (the summer house). At the time of the 1888 bicentennial celebration of Swedenborg's birth a new house had already been built on the Hornsgatan property, and on the ground between the buildings where Swedenborg's house and garden once stood, members of the New Church in Sweden and other countries have mounted a cast-iron plaque with Swedenborg's portrait in a bordered medallion. On this panel, the following words are engraved: "Venturus est tempus quando illustratio" (The time will come, when there will be enlightenment), taken from *Arcana Coelestia* 4402.[45] Starting in October 1986 extensive plans were made to reconstruct the entire garden together with the summer house.

The island of Djurgården east of today's central Stockholm was in Swedenborg's time a popular place for excursions, picnics and entertainment and remains so to this day. There is no doubt that Swedenborg visited this place often. Around 1890 great efforts were undertaken to make the island of Djurgården a center for the Swedish folk-culture, and to this end the open-air museum Skansen was founded. Its founder Arthur Hazelius, the son of a follower of the New Church, in collaboration with the New Church community decided to transport the old summer house— at the time the last remaining part of Swedenborg's estate—to the new open-air museum. This was in 1896.[46]

In 1960 the administrators of Skansen restored the summer house anew and in the process created a rose garden which was to have the greatest possible resemblance to the garden on Swedenborg's original property. But the house needed more and more repairs, and the financial support for this was then provided by the Swedish Swedenborg Society, founded in 1978, in collaboration with New Church Swedenborgian organizations in America and England. In September 1985, Swedenborg's house organ, which he used for private, meditative enjoyment, was also repaired. Now we can hear a concert of Swedenborg's time for ourselves, played by Mads Kjersgaard, organ restorer. Kjersgaard believes that this organ was made by young travelling journeyman in one of the organ shops in the vicinity of Swedenborg's residence on Hornsgatan.

At the end of July 1770, "after he had generously supplied his two servants," as F. G. Lindh put it, Swedenborg left Stockholm headed for Holland and England, especially for the purpose of publishing his work *The True Christian Religion.* He did not depart this world in the city of his birth, but in London, on the 29th of March, 17725

However, from this quiet corner in the Swedish capital the most important spiritual stimulus had already gone out into the whole world, and this process is certainly still going on.

Notes

1 Offene Tore (Swedenborg Zenter, Zürich) (3:2011): 158-170; translator, Kurt P. Nemitz.

2 In 1753, Sweden introduced the "new" Gregorian" calendar. It differed by eleven days from the old "Julian" calendar. According to our new calendar Swedenborg was born on the 9th of February.

3 Frans G. Lindh, " Swedenborg's Födelseort och Dop" (Swedenborg's Birthplace and Baptism), Nya Kyrkans Tidning (1914): 138.

4 F. G. Lindh, "Swedenborg som äktenskapskandidat" (Swedenborg as marriage prospect), Nya Kyrkans Tidning (1917): 41-43.

5 A street of this name.

6 A street of this name.

7 F. G. Lindh, "Swedenborg som Söderbo" (Swedenborg as living on Söder), Nya Kyrkans Tidning (1921): 137.

8 Cyriel Sigstedt, The Swedenborg Epic (London: Swedenborg Society, 1981), 97,162.

9 Carl Forsstrand, Linnés Stockholm (Linnaeus' Stockholm) (Stockholm: Hugo Gebers, 1915), 58-151.

10 Lindh, "Swedenborg som Söderbo," Nya Kyrkans Tidning (1921): 138.

11 P. D. A. Atterbom, Svenska siare och skalder (Swedish Prophets and Poets) (Örebro, Sweden: N. M. Lindh, 1863, Band 1), 13,48.

12 Arne Munthe, Västra Södermalm intill mitten av 1800 talet [Western Södermalm to mid- 19th Century] (Stockholm: Sancta Maria Magdalena Församlingshistoriekommité i och Högalid församlingar [municipalHistorical Commission for the communities of Sancta Maria Magdalena and Högalids], 1959), 313.

13 Quoted from manuscript in Fredrik Böök, Svensk Vardag [Swedish daily] (Stockholm: PA Norstedt & Söner, 1922), 85.

14 Sigstedt, chap. 31, 276.

15 Rudolph Leonhard Tafel, Documents conceming the Life and Character of Emanuel Swedenborg, Vol. 1,1875; Vol 2, pp. 647-666; 1890; Vol. 3, 1890.

16 C. C. Gjörwell, Anmärkningar i Sivenska historien (Comments on Swedish History), (Stockholm: NJ Nordström, 1786), chap. 26, 220-224.

17 The earliest report on the fire from Gothenburg is found in a letter of Immanuel Kant, which was published as an appendix to the Sewall-Görwitz translation of Träume eines Geistersehers in English (London: New

Church Press, 1899,1915).

18 The story was originally related in a letter from her grandson, Anders Fryxell, printed in Bernard von Beskow's, Minne öfver assesoren i Bergs-kollegium Emanuel Swedenborg (Memories of the Assessor of the Bergs Collegium Emanuel Swedenborg) (Stockholm: PA Norstedt & Söners, 1860), 108.

19 Kerstin Wickman, "Jobb för kroppsbyggare" (Work for a Bodybuilder), Stockholmstidningen (February 24,1982).

20 Lindh, "Swedenborg som Söderbo/' (1921): 138-140.

21 C. J. N. Manby, Swedenborg och Nya Kyrkan (Swedenborg and the New Church), (Stockholm: Nykyrkliga Bokförlaget, 1906), 38.

22 Sigstedt, chap. 39,492.

23 Carl-Göran Ekerwald, "Lusthus för andeskådare" (Summer home of a Spirit-seer), Vi 43 (October 23,1986): 13.

24 Lindh, "Swedenborg som Söderbo/' (1921): 145,146.

25 Henrik Alm, Emanuel Swedenborgs hus och trädgård (Emanuel Swedenborg's house and garden), Samfundet St Erifcs Årsbok 1938 (Yearbook of the Society of St. Erik 1938), (Stockholm: Wahlström k Widstrand, 1938): 162.

26 Carl Robsahm, "Robsahms memoirer öfver Swedenborg" (Robsahms memoirs of Swedenborg), Skandinavisk Nykyrkotidning (1876), 60, 74, 91, 105, 122, 137, 153, 170. Also published in Tafel's Documents, Vol. 1,30-51.

27 Documents, Vol. I, 40.

28 Documents, Vol. 1,47.

29 Tore Frängsmyr, "Wolffianismens genombrott i Uppsala" (The break-through of Wolffianism in Uppsala), Skrifter rörande Uppsala universitet C Organization och historia (Reflections on the University of Uppsala: Organization and History) (Uppsala: Uppsala Universitet, 1972, Vol 26), 136.

30 H. I. Carlson, Anmärkningar vid Herr Professor And. Fryxells skildring af Emanuel Sivedenborg (Notes on Professor And. Fryxell's description of Emanuel Swedenborg.) (Stockholm: Nya Kyrkans Bekännares Förlag, 1876), 2.

31 Harry Lenhammar, Tolerans och bekännelsetväng (Tolerance and forced confession), PhD Thesis (Uppsala: Uppsala University, 1966), 315.

32 Gjörwell, chap. 47, 220-224.

33 Tessin och Tessiniana: Biographie med anecdoter och reflexioner, sam-

lade utur framledne Riks-Rådet m. m, Greve CG. Tessins egenhändiga manuscripter (Tessin und Memorabilia: biography, anecdotes and reflections, compiled from the leading State Council, etc. Count C. G. Tessin's own manuscripts) (Stockholm: Johan Imnelius, 1819), 555,556.

34 Alm, 165.

35 Lindh, "Swedenborg som Söderbo", 1921:171,172.

36 Alfred Stroh, *Den Nya Kyrkan i Norden* (The New Church in the North) (Kopenhagen: Alfred Stroh, 1913), 9. See also Robsahm, 91. Docments, Vol. 1,36,37.

37 *Samlingar för Philantroper. I. Utdrag af några bref från Emanuel Svedenborg til åtskillige des vänner* (Collections of Philanthropists. Volume I. Extracts from some letters from Emanuel Swedenborg to Several of his Friends), Brief 10 (Stockholm: Exegetiska och philantropiska sällskapet, und A. J. Nordström, 1787).

38 Hjalmar Kylén, En Swedenborg Reformation i Sverige under första 1800-talsdecenniema (A
Swedenborgian Reformation in Sweden during the First Decade of the 19th century) (Stockholm:
F. C. Askebergs, 1910).

39 Sigstedt, 346-348. Jesper Swedberg, America illuminata (Enlighteried America), trans- lated and with an introduction by Robert Murray (Stockholm, 1985), in different places. An edition of Wallerius' Psychologia Empirica can be found in the library of the New Church, 4 Banérgatan, Stockholm, Documents, Vol II, 417-424,1158.

40 Documents, Vol 1,37, 627.

41 Inge Jonsson, Swedenborgs skapelsedrama "De Cultu et Amore Dex" (Swedenborgs Drama of Creation, The Worship and Love of God) (Stockholm: Nature och Kultur, 1961), 23, 24. Lenhammar, 256,380. Bror-Erik Ohlsson, Eskilstuna fristad (Freetown Eskilstuna) (Eskilstuna kommun III, 1971), 104. Olle Hjern, "Christian Johansén," Gnosis 1-2 (1986), 55.

42 Ekerwald, 13.

43 Alm, 167,168.

44 Ibid., 166.

45 "29 January 1888" Skandinavisk Nykyrkotidning (1888), 29.

46 The move is described by Alm, 171.

47 Lindh, "Swedenborg som Söderbo/'(1921), 171.

Carl Jonas Love Almqvist –
Great Poet and Swedenborgian Heretic

Olle Hjern

As my subject I have chosen the Swedish author, Carl Jonas Love Almqvist, and I have called him a great poet and a Swedenborgian heretic. I do not hesitate to say that he was a very great poet; but the question is if he really was a heretic. Perhaps we might call him that, but on the other hand I think that he in many ways had a deep vision of what had been revealed through Swedenborg, which could be of a real use for the New Church, to which he certainly can be regarded as belonging. It is quite sad that I can't translate for you all of his wonderful poems. There is hardly a single one translated into English. I remember the songs he has written like "The Awakening": how a person after death is waking up in the other world, how angels appear to him, how the mother, the father appear. It is in a language that is very, very touching.

Almqvist early declared concerning Swedenborg: "His relationship to the new life is the same as that of Christopher Columbus to America: the way to the new world, he showed, and all his accounts from there are truer. (This was in a letter to his friend Hazelius, the founder of the Open Air Museum, Skansen, in Stockholm, and I think very much reflects the ideas prevalent in Almqvist's circle.) In a letter to Henrik Öfverberg, he wrote: "Swedenborg is a spirit of strong innocence. As a teacher among men of heavenly things, he is the first point, the beginning of the new Time." In a work called Religion, religious customs, he stated that in the former Christian Church, the Lord revealed Himself in a material human shape, before the eyes of the body; but in the New Church He is revealing Himself also, but in an ideal Human Shape, before the vision of the spirit. And now it is the purpose that "man may come to envision the Lord, to see the Lord in a true Human Shape, in a Divine Human

114

Shape, as beautiful as is possible accommodated to one's spiritual state." The Lord Jesus Christ as the only God could be seen in the Divine Word if you had the real vision which united the heat and the light – if you had true internal experience of spiritual things, then you could see the Lord revealing Himself in the Word. What was essential, that those of the new religion should come to see. The formal, that must be there, but the formal must not rule over the essential.

And who was this man? Was he a well-known New Church man? He is certainly well-known in the literary tradition of Sweden that started already in the 18th century, and spread New Church ideas; in that century also, Carl Jonas Love Almqvist was born, in Stockholm, in 1793. (He died in Hamburg, Germany, in 1866.) Few writers have had their plays so often performed recently in Sweden as Almqvist, in spite of the fact that before the 1950's, none of his productions had been publicly performed. Many people have discovered a new world of beauty in his books, together with fascinating ideas with regard to social reform and with regard to the relationship between the sexes in human society.

When he was at the peak of his productivity, however, he experienced an enormous tragedy, by being accused of serious crime, never proved really, but the suspicions against him were there nevertheless, and one time strongly increased because of a book by a Swedish lawyer, Hemming Sjöberg, which was also translated into English, *A Poet's Tragedy* (1929). But the matter has been discussed again, and new material has appeared, and I think that my friend, Stig Jägerskiöld, who has published two books concerning this matter – he is an old professor of the history of law, historian and lawyer, who just half a year ago published a large book, *Innocence and Arsenic*, concerning these crime accusations – has fully convinced many including myself that Almqvist was entirely innocent; and even if not everybody would agree to this – because of the fact perhaps that he had certain business connections with persons who were not perfectly honest – it has nevertheless always been agreed that his greatness as a poet, novelist and social reformer remains untouched.

Most of his life he stayed in Sweden, in the Stockholm area or at Jönköping in the south, but shortly after the accusations against him, he went to America, where he stayed from 1851 to 1865, and from 1854 in Philadelphia.

Almqvist at first studied at the university, then worked as a private tutor, as a teacher, and as a headmaster of a well-known school in Stockholm, and very much as a journalist. In his childhood he had much contact with his grandfather, Carl Christoffer Gjörwell, a Stockholm librarian and writer who once, as you may know, made a fine description of his meeting with Emanuel Swedenborg, at which he wanted to find out the essence of Swedenborg's doctrinal beliefs.1 Gjörwell's account of his meeting with Swedenborg is made in quite an affirmative spirit, even though he was regarded as mostly inclined towards the Moravian faith.

It is also clear that at the Uppsala University, where Almqvist came as a young student, the teachings of Emanuel Swedenborg were very much discussed among the students there, especially among those from the Skara diocese of the Church of Sweden or from the province of Västergötland, which was about the same geographically. Close to this time, two "Swedenborgians" from this district were teaching there, Sven Lundblad, professor of theology, and Gustaf Knös, professor of oriental languages. Professor Knös, certainly a friend of Almqvist's, rather strongly defended the idea that the New Church in Sweden in the future should be built up within the frame of the established one; but there were very differing opinions concerning that. The main influence in making young Almqvist thoroughly interested in the writings of Swedenborg seems to have been his fellow-student Pehr Hemming Odhner, also from Västergötland, son of the first translator of the work *True Christian Religion*, Sanna Kristna Religionen, into Swedish, published in Copenhagen, Denmark, in 1795, and grandfather of Carl Theophilus Odhner, who came over here and became a central figure of the Academy. Pehr Hemming Odhner himself was also a Swedenborg translator, and later on he became one of the more prominent "Swedenborgian" clergymen within the Church of Sweden.

But of course, Almqvist must have heard about Swedenborg from his grandfather Gjörwell, and also from his uncle, Erik Abraham Almqvist, who was also a professor of theology at Uppsala and very much in favor of Swedenborg's writings, especially the doctrine of the Lord, the only God, Jesus Christ, which he expressed in several writings; and he later on became Bishop at Härnösand, in north Sweden. And also, in fact, Love Almqvist's grandfather was a professor of theology. He wrote a book which was very much used as a textbook, in Latin (we have some copies in Stockholm). It has the external form of a reply to certain questions put by the German scholar, Ernesti, who also as you may know had some- thing to do with attacks against Swedenborg. But it was really a review of the whole Christian dogma, and there were also some very good statements about Swedenborg's theology and Swedenborgianism; and this is one of the first times it was ever expressed that the Swedenborgians regard Swedenborg's later writings as "the Word," and then there is a reference to August Nordenskiöld's "Church Order," where the idea of the "Latin Word" was expressed and certainly, Love Almqvist was well acquainted with this idea, which was very much discussed in these circles. And I think that he also had the idea that the New Church could be realized, and he as it were tried in his thinking all the three ways, first, that the New Church should be built up within the established one, and also that it might form separate societies as it was stated in Nordenskiöld's "Church Order" and as was done in the Moravian societies, and also that it might be formed as associations or colonies according to these Utopistic thinkers like Fourier.

But after this time, the revelations to Emanuel Swedenborg certainly became the inmost spiritual guide for Almqvist, which stamped his whole life and everything which he wrote. You can't really say that he was influenced by Swedenborg: his identity as I am convinced was from the beginning to the end to be a prophet of the New

Church, in a certain way. Even if it can't be denied that under pressure, he sometimes defended his beliefs in a strange way, still there is no doubt that it was a main purpose of everything he wrote to bring forth the message of the Lord in His second coming, as he had understood this. He was also one of those who brought the Swedenborg publishing society "Pro Fide et Caritate," which had been founded in the 18th century, into life and activity again. He joined this society in 1817 and soon became its president, but was not quite satisfied with its activity. He was fully active in supporting the printing of Swedish translations of *Heaven and Hell*, of the early volumes of *Arcana Coelestia* and other works; but more than others in this society he wanted to form discussion circles on doctrine, theology and culture in general. And in connection also with this society, some of his friends arranged New Church services in the center of Stockholm, which he probably attended.

In 1817, he started within "Pro Fide et Caritate" "Mannasamfund" ("Society of Men"), in which the acknowledgment of Jesus Christ as God was fundamental; and they discussed the coming of the New Age and all that might involve. In "Pro Fide et Caritate" Almqvist read expositions of the Gospels in accordance with the teachings of Swedenborg's *Arcana Coelestia*. In the descriptions about the land of Canaan and the coming of the Lord there, he saw the opening of the internal man and the key to the understanding of ancient religious documents. It is rather clear that already now he expected that the Lord in this New Age would come with enlightenment to truly sensitive people within all fields of human development and culture.

One of his works from this time is *Murnis*, an account of life in the other world, in a very poetical and even sensual language, but literally fully in agreement with all the descriptions of the spiritual world in Swedenborg's writings; and there is a very deep tenderness in the description of how loving couples meet, their ruling love is gradually being discovered, and certainly in a poetical language. There is something of an atmosphere of deep piety, a warm sphere of love is prevailing among the angels described, there are also the angels who take care of small children who come there, an atmosphere of innocence and love; and here Almqvist for the first time is emphasizing the great importance of true conjugial love. This was to be something central in his literary production during the rest of his life. In Sweden, Murnis has often been regarded as the most "typically Swedenborgian" among Almqvist's works, and it is sometimes said that then he started more to emphasize practical matters – but of course he never gave up this first vision of heaven; it is always there. I think you could also say that he grew in his understanding of the New Church religion, that this was a matter of life, a matter of use, and therefore he became interested in social reform and also the problem of love-relations, marriages; and the solutions which he later on sometimes suggested did not always agree with those of his New Church friends, but no one would deny that he seriously struggled to solve such problems, according to what he saw revealed in the work *Conjugial Love*, even if he always wanted to point out that he was looking to the essence of the teachings in the first place, not primarily to the form. Swedish commentators sometimes claim that he wanted to have remedies for his own (as they believed) unhappy marriage, but this certainly cannot be anything very important in this connection.

The ideas must essentially have been there even before his own marriage, which took place in 1824 and started with great mutual expectations. It was when Almqvist and a group of fellow-believers had decided to try to build a "heaven on earth," to form a community in the countryside of the Swedish province Värmland, to lead a very simple and truly charitable life, to live among farmers, and as much as possible to enjoy the fresh nature of the Lord. They studied the work *Arcana Coelestia* together, found that Cainism, pictured within the sophisticated and purely externally refined life of human cities, had to be shunned in order that something of the life of the most ancients might appear. What was written concerning the most ancients, the Adamic state, was always a subject of Almqvist's interest – and also the "gentiles" – that was the genuine essence of people, which had to be restored. They wanted as much as possible to have contact with this Adamic essence in people, fully convinced that they would find unperverted and innocent people among those truly simple ones who lived away from the cities, and that they would change themselves in the good direction in this new environment. Then also, Almqvist married a charming girl, totally uneducated, but as he thought, representing the genuine people. But after two years the enthusiasm for these plans was entirely gone, and the whole group moved to Stockholm again. But certainly, many ideas had appeared there, and some of the people gathered there became very prominent people in the country, and it is said that perhaps the Swedish school system for all children was born during discussions at that place.

Carl Jonas Love Almqvist thus clearly was part of the, by necessity, poorly organized New Church movement in Sweden, where nevertheless many hard discussions and controversies occurred. It was strictly forbidden to separate from the established Church; but several New Church people had the idea that this should be done as soon as freedom would come, and one of them, Mårten Sturtzenbeeker, had that idea, but he had also other ideas which were rather controversial; and which in many ways were something which would be better understood in the future. He published a pamphlet called "Consolation for the criminal," "Tröst för den brottsliga," in which he in a very strange way deviated from what you could call New Church orthodoxy, by the idea that even crime is in a certain way in the Providence of the Lord: and that, I think, Almqvist did not agree with, but he agreed to the idea of a merciful treatment and an education of criminals – not that society should take revenge. It should help those in such difficulties.

I can continue especially to emphasize this matter of marriage, which was very very central. It appears in most of his novels. We have the work *Amorina*, which has often in recent years been performed at leading theaters in Sweden. The central person there, the girl Amorina, is a representative of the genuine religiosity which might appear among truly and in the very best sense simple, people. The worship of the Lord Jesus Christ as God and the belief in the spiritual world, "in the Swedenborgian spirit," as it is often said, is there throughout. Just the same might apply to the play *Drottningens Juvelsmycke*, The Jewels of the Queen, performed in the fall of 1987 until the beginning of 1988 at the National Theater in Stockholm in connection with its anniversary. According to Almqvist, the genuinely simple people were close to the celestial angels.

The ideas of conjugial love are to be seen everywhere here, but according to Almqvist, true marriages, marriages in a new religious spirit, might change the whole world and establish a kingdom of God already here on earth. In this new age, he thought, the spirit of true conjugial love was descending from heaven, and here on earth it was only too often ruined by formalism and hard compulsion by external bonds. In Almqvist's novels, which were very popular reading in Sweden during his lifetime, the loving couples generally find each other and solemn marriage rites and weddings are common. But nevertheless, the problem of the realization of a true marriage in our human society remains. Without freedom for correcting mistakes and dissolving purely formal marriages, he did not see any solution. At the same time he emphasized the family responsibilities of each one. "When a heavenly friendship is alive between two hearts so purely, so truly, so profoundly, so mightily that even if there would be some dissimilarity otherwise between them, this would be so small and subordinated that it would be joyfully burned away in the clear fire of friendship – then the souls of these creatures have been joined as a true couple, husband and wife." And in an opposite case, it does not help, if "the hand of a third person has blessed them." (Quotations from the novel *Baron Julius K.*) In some other novels, Almqvist again brings up the question if it might be possible for a person to have true marriage love more than once in life. His answers then are almost literally taken from Swedenborg's *Conjugial Love*. Thus in a certain way this might be possible, but it differs with each person, and this love would then never be on the same level. Then he published the novel *Det går an* (It might be permitted), which caused a big scandal and made his continued work with the schools practically impossible. This book describes a couple which among other reasons because of the dangers of formalism and external compulsion desists from any marriage rites by the Church or human society. Like several of Almqvist's other books it is a description of a journey. This couple is then passing by a place where a prominent lady lives who had been spreading and lending to the aunt of Sarah Rydebäck (the couple is Sarah and Albert) profound religious works. This lady is a real person, Anna Fredrika Ehrenborg, one of the very best New Church writers in the 19th century, and who did much to spread Swedenborg's writings and New Church literature, always in close contact with the organized New Church abroad; and she became the real founder of the organized New Church there, as it still remains. She was a very close friend of Love Almqvist. But Almqvist's book was regarded by the Church establishment and even by some of his fellow-believers, as a crime in itself which could not be excused. The book appeared in 1839.

Two years before, after much hesitation and against the advice of some of his friends, he had accepted being ordained by the Church of Sweden and having a partial work as a military chaplain. He claimed that it might be possible to work for the New Church within the frame of the old and established one. This of course did not make his situation easier. It should be remembered, however, that many situations in his novels were written there in order to illustrate applications and tentative interpretations of what was written in the work *Conjugial Love*, also what was written in the last part of this work, and not in the first place to advocate a practical program. But in the current case, in connection with *Det går an*, however, he wrote newspaper articles clearly defending the controversial ideas and claiming that they were essentially the same as those of Swedenborg, but certainly no one would emphasize monogamy and faithfulness for life as much as Almqvist and he was certainly not against marriage rites; but he thought that marriage laws should be in conscience, not in external bonds compelling.

About the same time Almqvist published the play, Marjam, concerning the virgin Mary, entirely in agreement with the writings of Swedenborg but in much conflict with Lutheran orthodoxy. The work was probably primarily inspired by Swedenborg's vision of Mary which was recorded in the work Continuation Concerning the Last Judgment. Here Almqvist made Paul a representative of the faith alone teachings which he intensely hated and attacked his character throughout. In the defense of this work he strongly claimed that the epistles were not the Word of the Lord like the four Gospels; and if they should be regarded as the Word, Swedenborg's and perhaps other writings certainly should be regarded as the Word, he declared - which was very hard for the Lutheran Church government in Sweden to take. And he emphasized instead of Paul, John, the apostle John, the Gospel of John, as the real Christian. He regarded John as representing the true Christianity which was spiritual, but also devoted to use in the world.

As a clergyman, Almqvist while still in Sweden was not defrocked but he could not continue his work in the schools. Now he had to be more active as a journalist, and he began frequently to contribute articles to the most radical newspapers, such as "Aftonbladet" in Stockholm and "Jönköpingsbladet" at Jönköping. He was most concerned with the problems of poverty and social injustice and strongly advocated a democratic government in the modern sense. He was quite close to those people in Sweden who propagated Swedenborgianism and socialism at the same time. Human society as a true neighbor according to the teachings of Swedenborg was something essential to him. And as love and wisdom, good and truth equally were the essential things of true religion, it had by all means to be emphasized that women and men must be fully equal in any human society. He was very far from ignorant of the differences between female and male natures but thought that these would appear in the best way when all rights in human societies would be fully equal for both women and men. Especially essential he regarded a balance of equality without any oppression whatever within marriages in this world.

Politically, Almqvist often appeared to be very radical, even socialistic, but as has often been pointed out, he was always working toward a "religious Utopia," a New Jerusalem on earth, centered upon true Christianity. In one of his late novels, *Tre Fruar i Småland*, Three Wives in Småland, he is expressing admiration for the phalanx society according to Fourier, which certain American Swedenborgians regarded as the true form for the New Church. It is quite possible that Almqvist for some time had the same ideas about this.

Very few people have ever been more optimistic than Carl Jonas Love Almqvist with regard to the potentialities of the revealed teachings to penetrate the whole of human society. The ancient and exotic myths should be interpreted according to the new knowledge of correspondences. The remains of gentile innocence with primitive people gave him hope that the spirit of the most ancients, the Adamic race, might return among men on earth. He was very interested in what he found was said in Swedenborg's writings concerning the ancient Word, hidden somewhere in Asia. And he devoted himself also very much to writing concerning the history of mankind and its applications to us of this time, and concerning gentiles. The original Adamic time and the time of the fall, the time of Cain, he saw pictured in myths and legends all over the world, and he described this in his work, The Legend of Mankind (*Menniskosläktets saga*), of which he unfortunately only published the first volume. And here he has interesting etymologies: he has the idea, for instance, that the ancient Scandinavian god Baldur is the same name as Baal, that is, when religion deteriorated. A sign that the religion had deteriorated was the introduction of human sacrifice – and in the Christian religion, of the terrible doctrine of the vicarious atonement by the Son to appease the wrath of the Father, which he regarded as one of the worst things.

The time of Cain, to Almqvist, was the time of human kingdoms, of oppression, the time of formalism and of slavery. It was the time of external form, not of internal essence. Now he was looking forward to the time when the essence of genuine love would return within the human forms, together with new rational enlightenment from

124

the Lord. Certain of his pages also picture a most intense personal piety, "mystical" in the very best sense.

Very often the discussion of ideas and problems of the time in Almqvist's works takes place in an imaginary "academy," "Mr. Hugo's academy," i.e. within a group of people gathered at a country manor house.

Almqvist now and then had serious financial problems, but he also often had a remarkable ability of settling them. He was not uninterested in business activities, sometimes enjoying reasonable successes. But his contact with Johan Jakob von Scheven, a former army officer who had become a rather well-known usurer in Stockholm, did not turn out well. Von Scheven was also a Swedenborgian, a New Church believer, close to the Rev. Johan Tybeck. After Tybeck's death Almqvist became his spiritual adviser who assisted him especially in studying those of Swedenborgs writings which had not yet appeared in Swedish. In the beginning they seem to have had a very fine contact, but when Almqvist had started to assist him also in his financial transactions, new problems arose. The old von Scheven seems to have turned senile and very suspicious. He had many people, even quite strange people, around, but it is clear that his whole archives of receipts was in a total mess. He had difficulties in remembering what he had settled and not settled, what he had kept and what he had lost. He also started to fear that someone would poison him.

Two younger women, both somewhat strange, were living with him in his house, and for quite a time they had both been aware of von Scheven's suspicions about theft of receipts or debt obligations or attempted murder by poison. Almqvist was in close contact with von Scheven's son, and when they feared that von Scheven was losing his sanity, he wanted his wife and their son to move into the house to take care of the old man. The other ladies in the house must have been very irritated about this, as they had been by the suspicions of the old man, evidently sometimes pointed at them. Almqvist was accused of dishonest handling of the financial matters, and one day one of the ladies reported that they suspected him of having put arsenic into the old man's soup. In spite of the lack of any real evidence or any motive (and even the fact that von Scheven was not poisoned, but lived on quite a healthy person to a good age), these accusations were taken seriously by the public. What made the situation worse was the discovery of certain private notes in Almqvist's home in which he had written how he should face the situation if the old man died, and how he should face it if he did not. (Someone in the Stockholm police had heard the rumors about Almqvist and reported him, not the von Scheven family nor the women in the house.)

Now Almqvist felt he had to leave Sweden for America. He arrived in New York, and after some stay there, he travelled around extensively, until he settled down in Philadelphia. Most of the time there, he seems to have resided at a boardinghouse on Walnut Street, later on Arch Street. He was a frequent visitor to the libraries. The details of his life there are quite obscure. Not the least his relationship to Emma Nugent, the head of the boardinghouse, seven years older than himself. He must have worked as a teacher of languages and music, and at the same time partially as a journalist for American and Swedish papers. He wrote a lot, and recently his work, *Om Svenska Rim*, On Swedish Rhymes, written there, was published for the first time.

We know that some of his well-known friends were the Rev. William Benade, and also the pharmacist and homeopathic doctor, F. E. Boericke, to whose address personally or to the company of Boericke and Tafel, all his mail from Sweden was sent. He writes home about Benade, "Here are even two Swedenborgian churches. One of them I have been attending, and the minister there, Mr. Benade, is an excellently nice fellow, in a certain way reminding me of Manne Olde." Emanuel Olde was one of Almqvist's early New Church friends in Sweden, later a language professor at the Lund University.

Benade and Almqvist must have had very much in common. In the past, both had had contact with the Moravians, and what was in the very center in Almqvist's whole literary and practical activity was a search for the right approach to a genuinely New Church

126

education, to establish a new society in the sphere of the new revelation, the Second Coming of the Lord. Perhaps he mentioned to Rev. Benade that he had written in his novels about an "Academy" of prudent people which might be a central circle for such efforts. Perhaps they discussed what might be the right form for this in America – but surely then Almqvist would have repeated: the right essence is the most important!

Carl Jonas Love Almqvist left Philadelphia in 1865, wanting to return to Sweden, where he had his family; but on the way home, he died.

Notes

1   R. L. Tafel, Documents Concerning Swedenborg
    (London: Swedenborg Society, 1890), 2, pp. 402-5.
2   Emanuel Swedenborg, Continuation Concerning
    the Last Judgment, no. 66; True Christian Religion, no. 102.

THE INFLUENCE OF EMANUEL SWEDENBORG IN SCANDINAVIA

OLLE HJERN

Outline:
I. Theology and Philosophy
  a. The Spread of Swedenborgianism
  b. The Effects of Swedenborgian Doctrines
  c. Publishing and Philanthropy
II. Arts and Letters
  a. The Romantic Period
  b. Strindberg
  c. Ekelund
III. Denmark and Norway
IV. Swedenborgian Influence in Recent Times

Beginning in the years of his youth, Emanuel Swedenborg sought recognition on that international stage where the boisterous drama of the Enlightenment was in progress. He offered the scientific works of his early period to Europe as a whole; and when his interest shifted to theology, he continued to reach out to readers beyond the borders of his native country. It is a testimony to the success of his efforts that he influenced thinkers far beyond Sweden, and that in recounting his influence today we must discuss intellectual trends not only in Europe but in points far beyond that continent.

Yet despite his international orientation, he left his mark on Sweden and the larger Scandinavian community as well. Here, however, it has often been said that his influence was primarily that of a writer influencing other artists of the written word. As I hope to show in this brief sketch, that influence on the writers of Scandinavia was real and persists to this day, but it is not the only impact Swedenborg had on the region. Accordingly, I will begin my observations by looking at his effect off theology and philosophy. Though Sweden is the primary focus of my attention in this essay, I will make some digressions to other Nordic nations.

I. Theology and Philosophy

One obvious reason that the artistic influence of Swedenborg in Scandinavia appears greater than his theological influence is that in his day a rigid censorship by the Lutheran state church existed in Sweden for all books of theology. It was easier to get approval for works of a Swedenborgian bent than for the works of Swedenborg himself. Even as early as 1766 the consistory of the Göteborg diocese approved a book of sermons that is undeniably Swedenborgian, written by Swedenborgs close friend Gabriel Beyer (1720-1779).[1] Some of the Göteborg clergy immediately and strenuously opposed this authorization with legal action, but a considerable group of laypeople in the city supported Swedenborg and those who were friendly to him.[2] As Göteborg was the center for the activities of the Swedish East India Company, the presence of a strong Swedenborg faction there encouraged the wider dissemination of Swedenborgian ideas.

a. The Spread of Swedenborgianism

Despite the ban of the state church, Swedenborgs writings gradually became available. That he wrote in Latin was both an impediment and an aid to the spread of his work: it restricted his audience to the educated and it relieved offlcial anxiety that his writings would corrupt "simple folk. "[3] His appeal was extended by several early translations made by Carl Fredrik Nordenskjöld (1756-1828), Jonas Pehrson Odhner (1744-1830), Christian Johansén (about 1746-1813), and others, printed in Copenhagen or circulated in handwritten form throughout western Sweden and Finland (at that time a part of Sweden).[4]

These early days were times of great contradiction. The estate of the clergy in the Swedish diet resisted Swedenborgs message, fearing

129

a schism in the Lutheran Church of Sweden; while the king, Gustav III (1746-1792), actually supported the printing of Swedenborgs works in Denmark, as did his brother, Charles (1748-1818), both as prince and later as King Charles XIII. Charles, in fact, attended at least one meeting of the *Exegetiska och Philantropiska Sällskapet* (Exegetical and Philanthropical Society), a Swedenborgian printing organization founded in 1786 after a gathering of Swedenborgians took place at Varnhem. This society counted some 150 of Swedens elite among its members, including Baron Leonhard Gyllenhaal (1752-1840) and Count Claes Ekeblad (1742-1808). Although it was shortlived, becoming entangled in shady projects in animal magnetism and gold making, it was followed by another, more sound society that upheld the scholarship and spiritual interests of Swedenborg, *Pro Fide et Charitate* (On Behalf of Faith and Charity).

Meanwhile, in Göteborg the vigorous opposition of the orthodox Lutheran circle soon overwhelmed the Swedenborgian element. Though as the second city of the nation Göteborg has in a sense remained a nexus of Swedenborgian activity within Sweden, the main focus of the Swedenborgian movement shifted to the neighboring diocese, Skara. Swedenborg had of course a historical connection with this region, having lived there when young with his father, Jesper Swedberg, the bishop of the diocese. Even during Swedenborgs lifetime "Swedenborgianism" was much discussed in Skara; there, as in Göteborg, one main point of dispute was Swedenborgs rejection of three separate persons in the Trinity, and in connection with that his further denial of the idea that Christ effected vicarious atonement for human sin.[5] Swedenborg himself viewed this anti-Trinitarian doctrine not as his invention but as a fundamental fact of proper Christian belief. Concerning the discussions of this topic at Göteborg, he wrote:[6] "There they call this Swedenborgianism, but I for my part [call it] "true Christianity". All the same, he never called for or supported the founding of a separate church to foster this change in doctrinal outlook, particularly not in his own name.

A large number of the clergy in Skara became open to Swedenborgs view of the Trinity, although they remained within the Church of Sweden. Arvid Ferelius (1725-1793), who had been Swedenborgs pastor during his final days in London, returned to Sweden an ardent believer and proselytizer; his three sons-in-law eventually became members of the half-secret *Pro Fide et Charitate.*[7] The dean of Skara, Anders Knös (1721-1799), in time acknowledged that he was a disciple of Swedenborg, and the unofficial movement grew to include bishops and professors of theology.[8]

Political changes in 1809 brought increased freedom of the press, and it thereafter became easier to print and distribute within Sweden works deviating from orthodox Lutheran doctrine. The new freedom soon bore rich fruit through one of the sons of Dean Knös, Gustav (1773-1828), who was a professor of what were then called oriental languages at the University of Uppsala and a mystic in the Swedenborgian tradition. His book *Samtal med mig sjelf om werlden, Menniskan och Gud* (Talks with Myself Concerning the World, Humankind, and God; 1827) stoutly defended Swedenborgs theology, while simultaneously repulsing proposals for the establishment of separate New Church institutions – which in any case was still strictly forbidden.[9]

A later exemplar of the initial Swedenborgian movement in Sweden was Achatius Kahl (1794-1888), a scholar of Swedenborg connected with the University of Lund; he wrote a seminal work in four parts titled *Nya Kyrkan och dess inflytande på Theologiens Studium i Sverige* (The New Church and Its Influence on the Study of Theology in Sweden; 1847-1864), in which he documented the role of Dean Knös and others.

b. The Effects of Swedenborgian Doctrines

The activities of the Swedenborgian movement were in many ways successful. Swedenborgs teachings concerning the Lord, the Trinity, redemption, and the spiritual world were widely spread within the Swedish clergy. It would be difficult to ascertain exactly how many members of this body could be counted as holding Swedenborgian beliefs during the early 1800s. In particular, a common rejection of the idea of vicarious atonement produced a cohesive group of dissenters from the theology of the state church. All the same, most Swedenborgian ministers maintained a diplomatic stance toward their more orthodox counterparts, and so were generally tolerated. There was, however, one important exception: the Reverend Johan Tybeck (1752-1831), a zealous and provocative exponent who dispersed numerous pamphlets throughout the country, including some aimed at the less educated class. Though defrocked in 1819, he continued his activities until his death with an unbroken zeal, supported by Swedenborgians both within Sweden and abroad (Lenhammar 1966, 235-255; [Kahl] 1847-1864, 3:106-144). So powerful was the ultimate effect of this entire discussion that Bishop Esajas Tegnér (1782-1831) declared vicarious atonement "a butcher doctrine, a blasphemy against both God and reason" (Tegnér [1827] 1921, 401). To this day it is rare to find Swedish clergy who actively espouse this particular teaching.

As we look back on those times, we can see that the hymnals and catechisms also became a field in which Swedenborgians could find expression. Johan Olof Wallin (1779-1839) was the editor of the state church hymnbook of 1819, in use until 1939; it reverberates with Christian Platonism and Swedenborgianism. Arvid August Afzelius (1785-1871) composed a hymn to the Creator that has outlived the hymnals of his day, "Dig skall min själ sitt offer bära" ("My Soul Gives Sacrifice to You"; Wallin 1819, number 28). This work dates from the time when Afzelius was a member of *Pro Fide et Charitate* in Stockholm; if his testimony is to be believed, New Church services were held by the organization in the very early years.[10] Bishop Jakob A. Lindblom (1746-1819) proposed a catechism in 1810 that maintained that the Father, Son, and Holy Spirit were different forms of revelation of the one eternal God ([Kahl] 1847-1864, 4:88). A somewhat later catechism, by the Skara bishop Sven Lundblad (1776-1837), was entirely Swedenborgian (Lundblad 1825).

Similar ideas appeared in the study by Erik Gustaf Geijer (1783-

1847) titled *Thorild: Tillika en philosophisk eller ophilosophisk bekännelse* (Thorild: Also, a Philosophical or Unphilosophical Confession; 1820). Because of this world Geijer was actually prosecuted for heresy on the grounds that its account of the Trinity and the atonement of Christ was contrary to the teachings of the state church. According to Geijer, Christ's atonement was a reconciliation between God and humanity, a restoration of the broken bond between them, as made by God himself in his human form; and furthermore, God continues in his human aspect to fight evil on our behalf. In Geijer's view, Christ was divine love and wisdom in human form, a revelation of the ideal human, the true higher personality that can be realized in each human being – and in this world, not by necessity in the next. In his *Svenska folkets historia* (History of the Swedish People; 1832),[11] he claims that Swedenborg represents the true religiosity of the Swedish people in modern times, as did St. Bridget in medieval times.[12]

c. Publishing and Philanthropy

Despite the abiding interest in Swedenborgian theology, no separate New Church society could be formed in Sweden un til 1866 (Goerwitz 1894, 270). Furthermore, such societies have remained small in Scandinavia as a whole, though they have often had an influence larger than their size might suggest, serving as the nuclei of major publishing initiatives.

An example of this publishing effort, albeit an idiosyncratic one, is the Swedenborgian bookseller and publisher Per Götrek (1798-1876), This "first Communist in Sweden" distributed both Swedenborgian tracts (Götrek 1854) and the *Communist Manifesto.* Odd though he may be, he represents the hunger for justice and social welfare that Swedenborg often inspired in his Swedish followers.

It should be observed that the early restriction against forming independent church societies did not stop Swedes from putting their Swedenborgian principles to use in organizations that were at least nominally secular. The Norrköping Association, founded in 1779, was one of the earliest Swedenborgian organizations in the nation;

its goal was to create new societies in Africa based upon equal rights for all, without permitting slavery or participation in the slave trade.

In general, the Swedenborgians of Sweden were confirmed abolitionists and organized themselves to implement their beliefs. In 1787, the naturalist Anders Sparrman (1748-1820) and Carl Bernhard Wadström (1746-1799), one of the founding members of the Exegetic and Philanthropic Society, visited Mezurado (present-day Monrovia, Liberia) and began to propagate the idea of the district serving as a haven for liberated slaves. Under the leadership of Wadström, and in conjunction with August Nordenskjöld (1754-1792) and English abolitionists, Swedenborgians actually did found a colony at Sierra Leone in West Africa.[13] Though it held much promise, it survived only for a brief time. Others worked without the benefit of such organizations; for example, Governor Salomon Maurits von Rajalin (1757-1825), an acknowledged Swedenborgian, tried unsuccessfully to end reliance on the slavery system in the Swedish West Indian colony of St. Barthélemy.[14]

Swedenborgian theology supported women, too, in philanthropic endeavor. Frederika Bremer (1801-1865) found two aspects of Swedenborgs writings particularly influential: his emphasis on the importance of being of use to ones neighbor, and his insistence that women should be free of domination by men.[15] She traveled to America, most likely drawn to Swedenborgian contacts in New England; later the same interest took her to London. In America she studied social relationships, focusing on slavery and the preparation for the emigration of liberated slaves to Liberia in West Africa.[16]

Although, strictly speaking, ecumenicism may not be considered a component of philanthropy, it springs from the same source. Swedenborgians have contributed to striking advances in ecumenicism, following their leaders belief that the particular form of worship is not important, so long as the worshipper has the intention to live morally and do good.[17] The World's Parliament of Religions of 1893, initiated by Swedenborgians in Chicago, had immediate consequences in Sweden.[18] On the initiative of New Church minis-

134

ter Albert Björck (1856-1938), a close collaboration began among Björck, the Jewish rabbi Gottlieb Klein (1852-1914), the liberal Christian scholar S. A. (Samuel Andreas) Fries (1867-1914), and the young minister and student of religions Nathan Söderblom (1836-1931). The result was a congress that took place in Stockholm in 1897 (Björck 1898). Björck and Söderblom, who were close friends, formed an organization that can be said to have been the beginning of the movement for a religious dialog and ecumenicism as a whole within Sweden.

II. Arts and Letters

I turn now to Swedenborgs influence on arts and letters, though of course these fields overlap with philosophy and theology. The end of the 1700's, less than three decades after the passing of Swedenborg, marks the beginning of the romantic era.

a. The Romantic Period

During this time the irrational, the emotional, and the experience of beauty found a new meaning in human thought. Those following this new trend eagerly seized on Swedenborgs idea that all of nature was a "representative theater" of the spiritual world[19] and a testimony of the divine love and wisdom of the Creator. His work *Marriage Love*, with its teaching that neither spouse should dominate, and its promise of a higher form of marriage in the other world – a virtual melding of two souls into one angel – held immense appeal to men and women trying to redefine love between the sexes. It is easy to trace the influence of Swedenborg during this period because Swedish poets and philosophers of the romantic era were generally quite ready to acknowledge their sources.

One of the first Swedish romantics to incorporate Swedenborgs works into the romantic vision was Thomas Thorild (1759-1808), a brilliant philosopher and a disciple of Gabriel Beyer at Göteborg. During a stay in England, he had extensive contact with Robert Hindmarsh (1759-1835) and the New Church society then forming in

London. At Thorild's request, Hindmarsh published his small work, *True Heavenly Religion Restored* (1790), in which Thorild describes the wonderful beauty of both the earthly and the spiritual world, as revealed by Emanuel Swedenborg.

Another testimony to the sway Swedenborg held over the romantic imagination appears in the work of the two leading literary critics of the early 1800's, Lorenzo Hammarsköld (1785-1827) and P.D.A. (Per Daniel Amadeus) Atterbom (1790-1855). In literary magazines they proclaimed Plotinus (205-270) and Swedenborg the spiritual leaders of the new era.[20] Hammarskölds 1821 work *Historiska anteckningar rörande fortgången och utvecklingen af det Philosophiska Studium i Sverige* (Historical Notes Concerning the Progress and Development of the Study of Philosophy in Sweden; 229-246), demonstrates the part Swedenborg had come to play in Swedish philosophical enquiry and integrates his thought into the older models of Plato (427-347 b.c.e.) and Plotinus.[25] Atterbom, a professor at Uppsala University, published *Svenska siare och skalder* (Swedish Seers and Poets; 1862-1863), a massive work in which Swedenborg holds a central place. Atterbom focused in particular on *Worship and Love of God, Heaven and Hell,* and *Marriage Love,* surprising even Swedenborgians familiar with these works by his exposition of the beauty and wonder to be found in them.

Carl Jonas Love Almqvist (1793-1866) was, particularly in his younger years, almost the perfect type of the romantic. A poet and novelist, he embraced Swedenborgian thought early, in part because of his attachment to his grandfather, Carl Christofferson Gjörwell (1731-1811), who had met Swedenborg and written an account of him (Tafel 1877, 402-405). After his graduation from Uppsala University, he soon became the president of *Pro Fide et Charitate,* which at the time was involved in publishing Swedenborgs works in Swedish translation, in particular *Secrets of Heaven.* The records of his speeches at the meetings of *Pro Fide* show him absorbed with applying elements of divine revelation in the Bible to the journey of the human soul toward regeneration.[22]

In his works in general we are constantly confronted with the importance of maintaining a relationship with the spiritual world and the necessity for being useful here so that we can be useful as well in the next life.

Almqvists favorite among Swedenborgs works seems to have been *Marriage Love.* Almqvist often emphasized that the inner bonds that knit a couple together are far more important than any external rites; and although this is not a Swedenborgian idea in itself, it is consonant with Swedenborgs belief that ones true intention is what really matters, not the superficial practices that often paper over bad intentions. Many New Church members then opposed, and many of them now would still oppose, Almqvists radical views of marriage; but it should be noted that Almqvist was most concerned to stress that there can be no good marriage without perfect equality between woman and man. What is more, he advocated the same equality in social and professional fields.

Education, too, deeply interested him. As an active teacher and the author of a large number of school textbooks, he could be regarded as one of the framers of the Swedish system of elementary education.

Almqvist suffered an unfortunate reversal in 1851 when he was accused of fraud and the attempted murder of a moneylender and fled from Sweden, though it seems most likely that he was in fact innocent.[23] In Philadelphia, Pennsylvania, he found a group of New Church followers where he evidently felt at home, returning to Europé only in 1865, shortly before his death.

In the same circle of romantics as Almqvist was Bernhard von Beskow (1796-1868), the secretary of the Swedish Academy and the author of a fine though slim biography of Swedenborg. He maintained that "even if we, together with the followers of this seer, claim that there is nothing imaginary in Swedenborgs spiritual world, nevertheless it is highly poetical, just as is Plato" (von Beskow 1860, 61). He emphasized this poetical aspect in his correspondence with the great Finnish writer Johan Ludvig Runeberg (1840-1877), who was deeply influenced by Swedenborg and his ideas concerning the spiritual world (Hjern 1963a, 107). Von Beskows credentials as a romantic are impeccable; he was probably the only Swedish intellectual who was personally acquainted with Johan Wolfgang von Goethe (1749-1832), Friedrich Schlegel (1772-1829), and most prominent German writers of the time.

In Scandinavia

b. Strindberg

From our perspective, Swedish letters in the latter decades of the 1800s is dominated by August Strindberg (1849-1912). It is arguable that he has done as much as anyone to make Swedenborgs name known both within Sweden and beyond it. Though he doubtless knew of Swedenborgs works during his intermittent studies at the University of Uppsala, he did not study them intensively until his stay in Paris in the 1890S. Here the Swedenborgian novel *Seraphita* by Honoré de Balzac (1799-1850) had become something of a cult phenomenon in literary circles (Balzac [1835] 1970); intrigued, Strindberg soon found translations of Swedenborg in French by Antoine-Joseph Pernety (1716-1796), as well as *Abrégé des Ouvrages d'Ém. Swédenborg* (Abridged Presentation of Emanuel Swedenborgs Works), an old anthology by Jean Francis D'Aillant de la Touche (1744?-1827?) that was actually Balzacs main source.[24] He also had some contact with a New Church congregation at Rue Thouin in Paris (Hjern 1963b, 12).

To Strindberg, who at that point was wandering in a kind of personal underworld, Swedenborg was a guide as compassionate and knowledgeable as the fictitious Vergil in Dantes *Inferno,* who guided the poet through the circles of hell. Under the immediate influence of his first view into Swedenborgs theology, Strindberg wrote his own *Inferno* (1897), followed by the book *Legender* (Legends; 1898). In these autobiographical pieces, Swedenborg is mentioned on nearly every page. Strindberg wrote the former work in France and the latter after his return to Sweden, where he was

138

able to gain access to many more Swedenborgian texts.

Reading Swedenborg brought Strindberg a tremendous liberation from depression. He had been harassed by visions and by what Swedenborg describes as infestations of evil spirits; now that Strindberg had a spiritual explanation for these experiences, they were no longer threatening to him. However, it should be noted that his understanding of Swedenborg was quite idiosyncratic. Upon the publication of Strindbergs works on Swedenborg, the Stockholm New Church minister Albert Björck (whose ecumenical activities have been mentioned above) took Strindberg to task in a booklet titled *Swedenborg, Strindberg och det ondas problem* (Swedenborg, Strindberg, and the Problem of Evil; 1900). Björck criticized Strindbergs understanding of Swedenborg and suggested that the dramatist would gain immeasurably by a better comprehension of the theologian's message.

Over the years that followed his homecoming in Sweden, Strindberg turned again and again to Swedenborgs theological writings as explicative of human psychology and as the only compelling description of the spiritual world. He repeatedly echoed Swedenborgs summons to us to repent our egoistic and materialistic existence, making that theme a hidden motif in his many dramas. *Dödsdansen* (The Dance of Death) is a prime example (Strindberg 1901). In this play a couple cannot live together in harmony, and yet cannot achieve a separation from one another; they suffer from *odium conjugiale,* marriage hatred, a concept utilized as early as Swedenborgs 1742 work *Rational Psychology,* and dealt with indirectly in *Marriage Love* (1768), from his theological period.[25] Strindberg also studied Swedenborgs diaries, in both Latin and Swedish, where he found political notions that supported him in his animosity to dictatorship; these views were welcomed in the socialist circles in which Strindberg moved in his later years.

Ultimately Strindberg worked with his erstwhile critic, Björck, to publish the voluminous *En blå bok* (A Blue Book; 1907-1912), which is replete with Strindbergs thinking on Swedenborgian correspondences,[26] as well as with references to Swedenborgs writings.

Strindberg acknowledged his debt with an opening inscription that read: "To Emanuel Swedenborg, the teacher and leader, this book is dedicated by the disciple."[27]

c. Ekelund

The Swedish writer who took Swedenborgs message most to heart, perhaps, is Vilhelm Ekelund (1880-1949). Unfortunately, he is not well known outside Sweden. Though a poet, he primarily wrote books of philosophical aphorisms; he was both a mystic and a philosopher at once. His purpose is to lead us as readers to self-reflection and to encourage us to open our minds to an influx from a higher power, or, to put it another way, to understand through self-examination a sublime governance within ourselves. He supports our movement toward a new understanding of divine revelation, wherever we may find it. Although he constantly refers to Swedenborg in most of his works, one of his most remarkable is *På hafsstranden* (On the Seashore; 1922), in which the chapter on Swedenborg's experiences is of perennial interest.[28]

III. Denmark and Norway

Swedenborg has exerted an influence on Scandinavian countries outside Sweden as well, though this influence is little studied or appreciated. The early Danish role in the republication of Swedenborgs works has been noted already. Denmark was also a hotbed for proselytizers who wished to start New Church societies in Sweden in the 1800s. However, the first "Scandinavian" New Church society was formed not on Swedish soil, but in the Danish colony of St. Thomas, in the West Indies, in 1848 (Hallengren 1994b, 128-142).

Aside from their ecclesiastical interest in Swedenborg, the Danes have absorbed him, if indirectly, into their literature. The Danish writer Meir Goldschmidt (1819-1887), now best known for his controversy with the philosopher Sören Kierkegaard (1813-1855),[29] reflects Swedenborgs influence, as does Kierkegaard himself – or at least some scholars suggest as much (Bohlin 1925, 50-59, and Ru-

140

bow 1952). Goldschmidt often speculated about the origin of religion, and in 1862 he played on this in a dramatic piece titled *Swedenborgs ungdom* (Swedenborgs Youth). Johannes Jorgensen (1866-1956) wrote his early works under the influence of Swedenborgian symbolism (Jorgensen 1916, 80). The romantic poet and dramatist Ernst von der Recke (1848-1933) was a member of the New Church. Under the rubric of Danish students we should also include the many prominent New Church followers in Greenland. At Thule, for example, in the northern part of the region, the minister Gudmund Boolsen (1927-) began translating the works of Swedenborg into Danish in the early 1960s.[30]

In the 1900s, an important circle of Swedenborgian discussion was formed by students in Oslo, Norway, although the initial impetus for this gathering was the reading of the romantic poet and writer Henrik Wergeland (1808-1845). Norway is the original home of the man who can be considered the first truly Scandinavian New Church minister, Adolf Theodor Boyesen (1823-1916). Cosmopolitan, to say the least, he was trained in the United States and ordained in Britain by Jonathan Bayley (1810-1886) in 1871 as a missionary to Denmark. From 1876 on he worked permanently in Stockholm, becoming a diligent translator into the Scandinavian languages.[31]

IV. Swedenborgian Influence in Recent Times

The further histories of Swedenborgian influence in the separate Scandinavian nations did not coalesce until 1978, when the Scandinavian Swedenborg Society was founded. The Society has published a number of new translations; and as part of that renewed interest, scholarship on the topic has increased. In the latter part of the twentieth century, scholars at the universities of Uppsala, Lund, and Stockholm contributed many papers, dissertations, and book-length studies on Swedenborg. The dissertation by Inge Jonsson, *Swedenborgs skapelsedrama De Cultu et Amore Dei* (Swedenborgs Drama of Creation "On the Worship and Love of God"; 1961); and that by Harry Lenhammar, *Tolerans och bekännelsetvång: Studier i den svenska swedenborgianismen 1765—1795* (Tolerance and Doctrinal Unity: A Study in Swedish Swedenborgianism 1765-1795; 1966), are fine exemplars of the work of the later 1900's; they blazed a new path for their traditional disciplines. Jonsson contributed a postscript to balance my own introduction when Martin Lamms seminal 1915 biography *Swedenborg: En studie över hans utveckling till mystiker och andeskådare* (Swedenborg: A Study of His Development into Mystic and Visionary; 1987) was republished.

Recent works have brought Swedenborg studies into the new millennium, many of them outside the umbrella of the Swedenborgian organizations. One striking instance is the massive new biography by Lars Bergquist, *Swedenborgs hemlighet: Om Ordets betydelse, änglarnas liv och tjänsten hos Gud* (The Secret of Swedenborg: The Meaning of the Word, the Life of the Angels, and Life [or Service] with God; 1999b); another is the volume by a leading Swedish literary critic, Olof Lagercranz, *Dikten om livet på den andra sidan; En bok om Emanuel Swedenborg* (Poem about Life on the Other Side: A Book about Swedenborg; 1996). The latter was issued in Swedish and German, and mostly recently (2002) in English in the United States. Its unheralded appearance on the scene was a surprise to Swedish New Church members, and it went on to achieve a certain popularity. In fact, it can be said to have been more widely read and reviewed than any other single book about Swedenborg in Sweden.

The arts, too, continue to explore Swedenborgian themes. The great Swedish modernist poet Gunnar Ekelöf (1907-1968) owes much to Swedenborg, especially in his poem *En Mölna-Elegi* (A Molna Elegy; 1960). Scandinavian art has always been intrigued by the idea that spirituality suffuses the material world, from the painters of "emblematic" art in Swedenborgs time, to the impressionists and symbolists of the 1800s, on to moderns such as Jewish artist Ernst Josephson (1851-1906), whose work is in this sense Swedenborgian. Thus, too, Oskar Bergman (1879-1963), a great proponent of Swedenborgs writings, often claimed that he painted the spiritual world by painting the physical world as realistically as possible.

142

As for theater, the plays of Almqvist and Strindberg have already been mentioned; they occasionally undergo revivals. The dramas of Erik Johan Stagnelius (1793-1823) also bear the impress of Swedenborgs experiences.[32] As of this writing, Ingmar Bergman, the director of film and stage, is exploring Strindberg, and is reported to be a daily and devoted reader of Swedenborg.[33]

To summarize this long and fruitful engagement with the thought of Swedenborg in Sweden and Scandinavia as a whole, we could return to the suggestion that the history of Swedenborgs influence in the region is a story of one great writer acting upon others. Clearly, however, Swedenborgs effect is greater than this. He has been a catalyst not only for artists, but for philosophers and those pondering the meaning of their religion and their place on earth. In this respect there is no particular Swedish or Scandinavian model of Swedenborgian influence, but rather a parallel to the catalyzing effect one sees in other cultures, both in Europe and beyond.

Notes

1. See [Beyer] 1767.

2. Further sources are: Lenhammar 1966, 43-112; Sundelin 1886, 58-1x5; Berg 1891, 58-145, and separately paginated appendix 1-306; [Kahl] 1847-1864; and Acton 1948-1955, which covers this topic intermittently on pages 690-736.

3. People of simple heart and faith were in fact, the audience Swedenborg intended for his 1758 work *Heaven and Hell;* see §1 there.

4. For these early translations, see the following:
for Nordenskjöld, Swedenborg [1758] 1787;
for Odhner, Hyde 1906, entry 1934;
for Johansén, see Hyde 1906, entries 1511, 2472,
For other references to these translations, see Lenhammar 1966; New Church Collection; Falck-Odhner Correspondence; and Odhner Translation Manuscript.

5. For Swedenborgs view of the unity of God, see *True Christianity* 5-17; for his view of vicarious atonement, see *The Lord* 18, (It is customary to refer to passages in Swedenborgs works by section numbers rather than page numbers, as the former are uniform in all editions.)

6. Letter to Gabriel Beyer, April 12,1770; see Acton 1948-1955, 709. Translations in this essay are those of the author, unless the source cited is in English.

7. On Ferelius, see Lenhammar 1966, 272, and Ekman 1924,14.

8. On Anders Knös, see Lenhammar 1966, 114; Sundelin 1886, 172; and Josefson 1937, 100 and the following pages.

9. On the Uppsala Knös family in general, see Horn 1921 and Mansén 1993.

10. Afzelius became a great folklorist and a cataloguer of folk traditions; together with Erik Gustaf Geijer (see below), he published a highly regarded work on old Swedish folk songs (Afzelius and Geijer 1814-1816). See also Afzelius 1901 and Hjern 1964,102 and following.

11. Reprinted in Geijer 1873.

12. See Geijer 1873, 244. On his work in general, see [Kahl] 1847-1864,
    4:43,56, 58, 91, 92.

13. On Nordenskjöld, see Häll 1995, 19-226; on Wadström, see Wadström
    1790, 70-73,126-132, and Dahlgren 1915.

14. For general background, see Skytte 1986.

15. On the concept of use in Swedenborg, see below, pages 358-359. On
    the avoidance of domination in marriage, see above, pages 80-81; and
    for one possible example out of many passages that could be offered,
    see *Marriage Love* 248.

16. On Bremer, see Bergquist 1995, 85-107, and Hallengren 1998b, 34-37.

17. On Swedenborgs view of religions other than the Christian faith,
    see page 65 with note 28, as well as note 102 on page 304.

18. On the parliament in general, and Block 1984, 366-369.

19. See, among many other passages, *Secrets of Heaven* 3000, 3483:4, 3518:2.

20. Nilsson 1916,115-118; Atterbom 1814, columns 290-295.

21. On the influence of Swedenborg on Swedish philosophy, see Kylén
    1910,142-151.

22. Almqvists talks in the *Pro Fide et Charitate* meetings can be found in
    Almqvist 1926, 37-84.

23. On this controversy and Almqvist in general, see Bergquist 1993,
    44-46; Hjern 1988a, 88-89, and 1999a, 42-45; Lysell 1999, 4-10;
    and Wirmark 1999, 27-34.

24. For Pernetys translations, see Hyde 1906, entries 1108, 1109
    (with further reference to 3349), 1110, 1111, 2078, and 2079.
    For the translation of D'Aillant de la Touche, see Swedenborg 1788.

25. See *Draft of a Rational Psychology* §208. For an example see *odium* between
    partners in the work *Marriage Love,* see §292.

26. For more on correspondences, see pages 66 and 341-342 in Scribe of
    Heaven (2005).

27. Strindberg 1907-1912, title page of volume 1. On Swedenborgs
    influence on Strindberg in general, see Stockenström 1988,137-158;
    and on *A Blue Book* in particular, 138-139. Other relevant studies include

Stockenström 1972, Lamm 1936, and Berendsohn 1948.

28. On Ekelund and Swedenborg, see Andersson 1999, 33-37; Hjern 1999b, 197-200; and Bergquist 1999a, 209-222.

29. For the classic description of this controversy by a biographer sympathetic to Kierkegaard, see Lowrie 1938, 347-363. For an account in primary sources, see Kirmmse 1996, 65-88.

30. See Swedenborg [1758] 1971 (a translation of Heaven and Hell)\ [1758] 1978a (Other Planets); 1983-1995 (Spiritual Experiences); [1758] 1995c (Last Judgment); [1768] (Marriage Love); [1763] 1998a (Divine Love and Wisdom); and [1763] 1998b (Life and Faith).

31. For examples, see Swedenborg [1771] 1903 *(True Christianity; Swedish)*; and the following entries in Hyde 1906 (all in Danish): 983 *(Other Planets)*, 1103 *(Heaven and Hell)*, 1199 *(Last Judgment)*, 1275 and 1276 *(New Jerusalem)*, 1768 *(The Lord)*, 2024 *(Supplements)*, 2077 *(Divine Love and Wisdom)*, and 2799 and 2800 (both *True Christianity)*.

32. On Stagnelius in general, see Böök 1919; and Lysell 1993, especially after page 439.

33. Personal communication with the author by a member of Bergman's theater troupe. See also Sundgren 1998, 24, 27, 29-31.

Bibliography:

Acton, Alfred, *The Letters and Memorials of Emanuel Swedenborg.* 2 vols. Bryn Athyn PA, Academy of the New Church, 1948-1955.

Afzelius, Arvid August, *Minnen.* Stockholm, Norstedts, 1901.

Afzelius, Arvid August och Eric Gustav Geijer, *Svenska folkvisor.* 3 vols , 1814-1816.

Almqvist, JLA, *Samlade Skrifter.* vol. 2 ed. Fredrik Böök, Stockholm Albert Bonniers, 1926.

Andersson, Lars Gustaf, "Förälskningsmomentet" i Per Erik Ljung ed, *Den största Lyckan...* 1999.

Atterbom, PDA, "Recensioner" *Litteraturtidningen* 19 columns 290-295. Berg, Wilhelm, *Göteborgsstift under 1700 talet.* Göteborg, Wettergren & Kerber, 1891.

Berendsohn, Walter, *Strindbergs sista lefvnadsår.* Stockholm, Saxon och Lindström 1948.

Bergqvist Tillvarons hemlighet finns hos törnrosen" in Parnass 1993: 2. Reprinted in Världarnas möte: Nya Kyrkans Tidning 4-5: 15-20, 1999.

Bergqvist, Lars, "Swedenborg-Ekelund: Porträtt med dubbelexponering" i Per Erik Ljung ed. *Den största Lyckan...* 1999.

Bergqvist, Olle, *Om "Frälsarens dyra blod" och tidningsläsning hos Gud.* Skellefteå, Artos, 1995.

Beyer, Gabriel, *Nya försök till uppbygglig förklaring öfwer evangeliska sön- och högtidstexterna.* Göteborg, Lange, 1767.

Block, Marguerite Beck, *The New Church in a New World. A Study of Swedenborgiansim in America.* Enlarged edition, New York, Swedenborg Publishing Association, 1984.

Böök, Fredrik, *Erik Johan Stagnelius.* Stockholm, Bonnier, 1919.

Dahlstrand, Fredrik C. "Carl Bernhard Wadström, hans verksamhet för slavhandelns bekämpande och de samtida kolonisationsplanerna i Västafrika. Bibliogtrafisk sammanställning." *Nordisk tidskrift för bok och biblioteksväsende.* 1982.

Ekman, Hedda, *Två släkter.* Stockholm, 1924.

Geijer, Eric Gustaf, *Thorild: Tillika en philosophisk och ophilosophisk bekännelse.* Uppsala, Palmblad 1820.

Geijer, Eric Gustaf, *Svenska folkets historia,* in vol. 5 av Samlade Skrifter, Stockholm, P. A. Norstedt & söner, 1873.

Häll, Jan, *I Swedenborgs labyrint: Studier i de gustavianska swedenborgarnas liv och tänkande.* Stockholm, Atlantis, 1995.

Hallengren, Anders, "Swedenborgs väg till Boston", *Världarnas möte: Nya Kyrkans tidning* 3: 34-37, 1998.

Hjern, Olle, "Love Almqvist och Nya Kyrkan i Pennsylvania", *Världarnas möte: Nya Kyrkans tidning,* 4-5: 42-45, 1999.

Hjern, Olle, *"Religiositet och andlighet hos Vilhelm Ekelund"* i Per Erik Ljung ed. Den största Lyckan... 1999.

Horn, Vivi, *De små knösarna.* Stockholm, Geber, 1921.

Hyde, James, *A Bibliography of the Works of Emanuel Swedenborg, Original and Translated.* London, Swedenborg Society, 1906.

Josefson, Ruben, *Andreas Knös teologiska åskådning.* Diss. Univ. Uppsala, 1937.

Kahl, Achatius, *Den nya kyrkan och teologins studium i Sverige.* 4 vols. Lund, Bering, 1847-1864.

Kirmmse, *Encounters with Kierkegaard: A Life as seen by his Contemporaries.* transl by Bruce H. Kirmmse and Virginia R. Larsen, Princeton, Princeton University Press, 1947.

Kylén, Hjalmar, "Some indications on Swedenborg's Influence on Swedish and German Thought" in *Transactions of the International Swedenborg Congress,* London, Swedenborg Society, 1910.

Lamm, Martin, *Strindberg och makterna.* Stockholm, Svenska kyrkans diakonistyrelse, 1936.

Lenhammar, Harry, *Tolerans och bekännelsetvång: studier i den svenska swedenborgianismen 1765-1795.* Uppsala, Acta universitatis upsaliensis, 1966.

Ljung, Per Erik och Helena Nilsson eds, *Den största Lyckan: En bok till Vilhelm Ekelund.* Lund, Ellerström 1999.

Lowrie, Walter, *Kierkegaard.* London, Oxford University Press, 1938.

Lysell, Roland, *Erik Johan Stagnelius.* Stockhom / Stehag Brutus Östling, 1993.

Lysell, Roland, "Almqvist och Swedenborg" *Världarnas möte: Nya Kyrkans Tidning*, 4-5: 4-10, 1999.

Mansén, Elisabeth, *Konsten att förgylla vardagen. Thekla knös och romantiken.* Diss. Univ. Lund, 1993.

Nilsson, Albert, *Svensk romantik.* Lund, 1916.

Skytte, Göran, *Kungliga svenska slaveriet.* Stockholm, Askelin & Häggstrand 1986.

Stockenström, Göran, *Strindberg som mystiker.* Diss. Univ. Uppsala 1972.

Stockenström, Göran, "Strindberg och Swedenborg". In *Emanuel Swedenborg: A Continuing Vision* edited by Robin Larsen et al. New York: Swedenborg Foundation, 1988.

Strindberg, August, *De Blå böckerna* - A Blue Book, Ystad, 1907-1912.

Sundelin, Robert, *Swedenborgianismens historia i Sverige under förra århundradet.* Uppsala, W. Schultz, 1886.

Sundgren, Nils Petter, "I mästarens grepp", *Månadsjournalen* 3, 1998.

Swedenborg, Emanuel, *Abregé des Ouvrages d'Em. Swedenborg* prepared by D'Aillant de la Touche, Stockholm [Strasbourg] Exegetical and Philantropical Society, 1788.

Swedenborg, Emanuel, *Diary, Recounting Spirtual Experiences during the years 1745-1765.* 3 vols. Transl by John Durban Odhner, Bryn Athyn PA, General Church of the New Jerusalem. The first three volumes in English of Swedenborg's Latin Work *Experentiae spiritualis* edited by Johgn Durban Odhner, Bryn Athyn, PA, Academy of the New Church 1983-1997. Further volumes forthcoming.

Swedenborg, Emanuel, *Rational Psychology.* transl. Norbert H. Rogers & Alfred Acton, Bryn Athyn, PA, Swedenborg Scientific Association. Revision of 1950 edition, Philadelphia, Swedenborg Scientific Association, 2001.

Wadström, Carl Bernhard, Letter I and Letter II *New Jerusalem Magazine* 1790, 1: 70-73, 126-132.

Wirmark, Margareta, "Det går an – en sju dagar lång skapelseakt" *Världarnas möte: Nya Kyrkans tidning* 4-5: 27-34., 1999.

Bibliography:

On Emanuel Swedenborg, unpublished essay earlier available on Swedenborgsbiblioteket i Gröndal's homepage.

"En andlig väg och Svar till Swedenborg", *Världarnas möte: Nya Kyrkans tidning* 1991 nr. 1-2, pp. 2-16.

"Utomkroppsliga upplevelser i ljuset av Emanuel Swedenborg", Kersti Wistrand och Jan Pilotti (eds.), *Medvetandet och döden: En antologi om nära-döden-fenomen och utomkroppsliga upplevelser*, Stockholm, Natur och Kultur, 1982, pp. 82-96.

"Landskapet som själstillstand: Om Swedenborgs betydelse för Ivan Aguéli", *Aguelimuseets Årskrift* Årg. 24, 2011, pp. 16-20.

"Religiositet och andlighet hos Vilhelm Ekelund", Per Erik Ljung och Helena Nilsson (eds.), *Den största Lyckan: En bok till Vilhelm Ekelund*, Lund, Ellerströms, 1999, pp. 197-200.

"Skaraswedenborgianismen", Karl Erik Tysk (ed.), *Vetenskap, mystik och religion: den mångdimensionelle Emanuel Swedenborg*. Acta Bibliothecae Scarensis 10, Skara: Stifts- och Landsbiblioteket, 2000, pp. 56-61.

"Swedenborg in Stockholm" originally published in *Emanuel Swedenborg: A Continuing Vision* edited by Robin Larsen et al. New York: Swedenborg Foundation, 1988. Recently republished in *New Philosophy* January/June 2012, vol. 115. pp. 217-235

"Carl Jonas Love Almqvist – Great Poet and Swedenborgian Heretic", in Erland Brock et al. (eds.), *Swedenborg and his Influence,* Bryn Athyn: Academy of the New Church, 1988. pp. 80-90.

"Swedenborg and His Influence in Scandinavia" in Jonathan Rose, Stuart Shotwell and Mary Lou Bertucci (eds.), *Scribe of Heaven: Swedenborg's Life, Work and Impact.*, West Chester, Swedenborg Foundation, 2005. pp. 151-165.

ISBN 978-91-982096-3-1

© LNC Publishing USA
Editing: Dawn Potts & Gail Oler
Layout: Ottar Ludvigsen
Cover: Tanya Perskaya
Publisher: Edition TPW-Tornet
First Edition: 300 copies
Printing: BoD Germany 2019